UNDERSTANDING DYSLEXIA

T. R. Miles was educated at Winchester and Magdalen College, Oxford. He has been the Professor of Psychology at the University College of North Wales, Bangor, since 1963. He has written extensively on dyslexia and other subjects. He is married, with one son. He is an amateur 'cellist and a former Wimbledon lawn tennis player. He and his wife are members of the Society of Friends.

ISBN 1 871458 07 2

Previously published by
Batter Books (Publishing)

Published in January 1990 by

Bath Educational Publishers Ltd.
7 Walcot Buildings
London Road
Bath BA1 6AD

Printed by

Billing & Sons Ltd.
Hylton Road
Worcester WR2 5JU

Contents

		Page
Foreword Professor O. L. Zangwill		7
1 Four Case Studies		13
2 Recognising Dyslexia		40
3 Doubtful Cases		57
4 What Causes Dyslexia?		72
5 Problems of Screening		84
6 Dyslexia and Morale		87
7 Organising the Teaching		93
8 At the Secondary Stage		106
9 Into Adulthood		112
10 Recent Developments		124
References:	(i) Books and articles	137
	(ii) Tests	144
Appendix I	Recognising the Dyslexic Child	146
Appendix II	Suggestions for Further Reading	
	(i) General Background	151
	(ii) Research Reports and More Technical Books	152
	(iii) Teaching Books and Programmes	152
Glossary		154
List of Centres		156
Index of Names		157
Index of Subjects		158

Preface to the New 1987 edition

The following are the main changes which have been made.

The 1978 edition of this book has now been out of print for a number of years. Rather than attempt any extensive re-writing, however, it seemed preferable to let the existing material stand (since it has not ceased to be relevant), to supplement some of the chapters with further comments, and to write a single extra chapter (Chapter 10) designed to take account of recent developments. The further comments are identifiable by a small break in the text and by the date 1987 at the start of the next paragraph.

A reference section has been added so as to ensure that accounts of research findings are suitably documented and various changes have been made in the numbering and content of the Appendixes.

I am grateful to Howard Welchman, of Better Books (Publishing), for all his help with the preparation of the new edition.

T.R.M.
Bangor, 1986

Foreword

by O. L. Zangwill

AS every parent knows, children differ enormously in the facility with which they learn to read. While some seem to pick it up almost effortlessly, others, apparently no less intelligent, find it difficult and discouraging. Teachers, too, are very well aware of such differences, not only in learning to read but also in learning to spell which, for some slow readers at least, appears to present almost insurmountable difficulties. As a result, slow learners readily become sensitive and frustrated, especially when there are younger brothers. or sisters already showing signs of outstripping them in school progress. Reading, therefore, must be regarded as a skill which by no means every child of normal intelligence can easily master, no matter how well and patiently taught. Moreover, some children – fortunately only a very small minority – find difficulties with reading and spelling out of all proportion to their intellectual competence and in spite of every encouragement they have received from parents and teachers. Why is this? And, perhaps even more important, what can we do about it?

These are the questions to which Professor T. R. Miles addresses himself in this lucid and sensible book. As he makes clear, the book is concerned not with backward readers generally, but only with that relatively small proportion of them as may properly be called *dyslexic*, that is, those with severe reading problems which can be ascribed neither to overall lack of intelligence or educational opportunity nor to emotional or social difficulties at home or at school. As Professor Miles makes clear, these are children who, while in no sense physically or mentally abnormal, do in fact suffer from a genuine developmental handicap. Their disability is educational rather than medical in the ordinary sense.

This handicap was at one time known as 'word-blindness' and it is significant that some of the earliest reports of it came from ophthalmologists, who had obviously been consulted by the parents of dyslexic children in the belief that they might conceivably have been suffering from an obscure disorder of visual recognition. Although this may indeed be so, in some cases at least, there can be no doubt that the source of the disability lies not in the eye but in the brain. In consequence, the disorder has come to be regarded as in some sense neurological, though it is evident that it need not be associated with any obvious signs of brain injury. As Professor Miles quite properly suggests, dyslexia may best be regarded as 'constitutional', in so far as it is 'built into' the bodily constitution either through inheritance or possibly through the vicissitudes of development in the earliest years of life.

For this reason, the condition is often known as *specific* or *developmental dyslexia*. It is *specific* in so far as it is independent of intelligence or memory in general (although there are often associated features) and it is *developmental* in so far as it bears upon the acquisition of reading and spelling skills rather than upon breakdown of these skills after they have been acquired, as may occur in an older child or adult in consequence of injury or disease of the brain. Unlike many forms of psychological difficulty which may have a bearing upon education, in particular the neuroses and behaviour disorders which are the province of the psychiatrist, developmental dyslexia depends only in very minor ways upon external or environmental factors – though this is not of course to say that it is entirely unaffected by environmental influence. Indeed, the goal of helping dyslexic children through the development of teaching methods especially directed towards the overcoming of their special difficulties is obviously that to which research should be directed and clearly animates the writer of this book.

The earliest explanation to be given of developmental dyslexia is that it might be due to maldevelopment of a small part of the brain which is thought to be concerned with the acquisition and control of reading. Although damage of the area in question is known to disrupt reading in the adult, there is no evidence of any structural brain disorder in developmental dyslexia, though some more subtle impairment or 'lag' in its functional development may of course exist. It is unlikely, however, that the error can be traced to any very specifically localised mechanism (or what used to be called a 'centre') in a particular part of the brain.

A second explanation was advanced by an American paediatric neurologist, S. T. Orton, who was perhaps the first medical man to appreciate the educational implications of clinical neurology. Orton was much struck by the incidence of left-handedness and mixed hand-preferences among dyslexic children, as also by the incidence of reversal errors in their writing, and even occasionally in their speech. For these he coined the unaesthetic neologism *strephosymbolia* (literally, 'twisted symbols'). Strephosymbolia, which is of course common in the writing of young children, is shown in such errors as confusion of b with d or of p with q, and may involve reversal of the order of letters within a word, e.g. 'saw' for 'was'. But whereas such errors are soon eliminated by normal readers, they may persist for some years among dyslexic children and are eliminated only with much difficulty. Orton believed that these errors arise in consequence of competition between the two cerebral hemispheres in the control of reading and spelling, which he attributed to the lack of firm lateral preferences and in consequence to the failure of one hemisphere to achieve the normal exclusive control of language and speech. This hemisphere, normally the left, has long been known as the dominant hemisphere, and dyslexia could thus be ascribed to a failure to establish normal cerebral dominance.

Although Orton's theory is is many ways attractive, it

is, admittedly, very speculative. While left and mixed-handedness do occur very frequently in dyslexic children and their families, most left or mixed handed children learn to read normally and further factors must undoubtedly play a part. Furthermore, recent work has cast some doubt on the relation between handedness and cerebral dominance, and it now seems plain that the dominant hemisphere in most partly or even wholly left-handed individuals is the left, and not the right as was long supposed. Nonetheless, there is at the least a strong possibility that difficulty in learning to read and spell is linked in some way with the issue of cerebral dominance, though exactly what this relation is has still to be ascertained.

A third explanation – and the most popular today – is that dyslexia results from a retardation in the general development of language ('developmental lag') and that this handicap tends to run in families; in other words, its basis is genetical. Reading and spelling are acquired later and with greater voluntary effort than the acquisition of spoken language, and are accordingly more severely affected by this developmental handicap. As we now know, many (though not all) dyslexic children turn out to have been relatively slow in learning to talk, and as Professor Miles indicates, some residual difficulty in articulation or sentence structure may be apparent much later on, especially if it is looked for. Further, there is often residual difficulty in what one might call 'high-level' verbal activity, for example in written composition, in précis-writing, or on undertaking those tasks which psychologists refer to as 'verbal' intelligence tests. This need imply no general want of intelligence, merely a limitation in the intellectual uses and applications of language.

At the same time, the evidence for a genetical basis is still largely circumstantial. As Professor Miles points out, it is suggested by the frequent incidence of language retardation or reading difficulty in the family history of dyslexic children, by the far higher incidence of dyslexia in boys than in girls, suggesting a partially sex-linked factor, and perhaps by the not infrequent association of dyslexia with familial left-handedness, particularly, perhaps, in the mother. Unfortunately, the geneticists can still tell us nothing very precise about the inheritance either of left-handedness or of learning disability; in fact the position is just about as obscure as in the vexed problem of the inheritance of intellectual capacity.

It is still widely supposed that if the origin of a disorder, physical or mental, is 'genetical', that is inherited, nothing whatsoever can be done to alleviate it. Indeed theories of mental disorder based on the concept of an inherited predisposition are often dubbed fatalistic, the implication being that no treatment is possible. Nothing could be further from the truth. In our own time, we have seen one variety of educational subnormality (phenylketonuria) virtually eliminated by early diagnosis and correction through dietary means of an inborn error of metabolism. We have seen, too, much serious psychiatric illness which depends, at least in part, on genetical predisposition greatly relieved, and sometimes indeed apparently cured, by medication and environmental modification. In the same way, the fact that dyslexia has a constitutional foundation provides no reason whatsoever to relax remedial effort: it merely redoubles the need for it.

Although I have spoken of dyslexia as 'specific', this does not mean that it may not be associated with other features, which may or may not contribute to the central difficulties in reading and spelling. Indeed Professor Miles specifies a number of things, among them a tendency to confuse left and right; poor immediate memory for words, letters or digits – a factor which almost certainly contributes to the spelling difficulty; troubles in learning and reciting arithmetical tables and sometimes, too, a curious difficulty in retaining order of sequence which may lead, for example to using the correct letters in spelling a word but putting them in the wrong order. The extent to which these various difficulties are cause or effect of the basic trouble in reading and spelling has still to be determined. At all events, dyslexia –

to use a medical term – is better described as a 'syndrome', that is as a constellation of associated difficulties, rather than as a difficulty in reading and spelling in the narrow sense.

Although Professor Miles does not enter into details about methods of remedial education, he devotes considerable space to the organisation of teaching programmes for dyslexic children and to the very real – and sometimes heartbreaking – problems that so often afflict the parents of such children in connection with secondary education. This account is both sensible and wise and should be of considerable help not only to parents but also to remedial teachers who are specially concerned with designing courses to give assistance to the backward reader. Although awareness of dyslexia has grown appreciably in recent years, many Education Authorities are still unconvinced of its existence and its nature and implications are still very imperfectly understood.

One hopes that this book will be widely read and that its message will gradually filter through to all concerned with making the best of our educational potential in the challenging world of today.

Psychological Laboratory
University of Cambridge, 1974

1

Four Case Studies

THIS book is addressed to parents, doctors, teachers, administrators, psychologists, social workers, and indeed to anyone else who wishes to find out more about dyslexia. I shall introduce the subject by citing four case studies, all of which have been chosen in order to illustrate the difficulties experienced by dyslexic children. Chapters 2 and 3 are concerned with diagnosis and Chapter 4 with causation. Chapter 5 discusses problems of screening, Chapter 6 problems of morale, and Chapter 7 problems of organising suitable teaching. In Chapter 8 I indicate ways of helping the dyslexic pupil when he has reached the secondary stage, while in Chapter 9 I cite further case studies designed to illustrate the prospects for him as he grows up.

I shall not make any detailed suggestions with regard to teaching procedures since I have done this elsewhere (see Miles & Miles 1983). My main purpose will be to show how dyslexic children can be recognised and how provision can be made, both at school and in the home, for helping them.

No attempt will be made at detailed documentation of the views which I shall put forward, though confirmatory evidence is available in most of the references given on pp. 150–152. Any book of this kind must of necessity be based in some measure on the writer's personal experience, but I have tried not to depart in any serious way from the consensus of views held by those who take the concept of dyslexia seriously.

No two cases of dyslexia are exactly alike. Indeed, in view of the many kinds of variation which exist in nature, this is not surprising. Once one has seen a few cases, however, there emerges a clear basic pattern. Its essential features are: difficulty over learning to spell despite adequate opportunity and intelligence, difficulty over learning to read, difficulty in some tasks involving awareness of left and right, difficulty over arranging things in the correct temporal sequence, difficulty with certain kinds of items involving short-term memory, and sometimes difficulty over subtraction and difficulty in learning and reciting arithmetical tables. In the case of any particular skill a dyslexic child can learn to compensate for some of these difficulties; as a result of hard effort, for instance, he will probably become able to read more or less adequately, and even spelling may eventually not be too much of a problem. One is left in no doubt, however, that such a child has a handicap, and to judge his performance by standards appropriate to those without this handicap is bound to create unhappiness.

The four people whom I shall describe in this chapter – Henry aged 10, John and Laura both aged 15, and Robert aged 19 – can, I think, be regarded as typical cases of dyslexia in almost all respects. Admittedly it is possible to be less severely handicapped than they were, and the handicap can be less crippling when special teaching is arranged at an earlier age, preferably by the time the child is aged 8. Between them, however, these four cases seem to me to provide a clear illustration of the problems which a dyslexic child is likely to meet in the present educational system, particularly if his dyslexia is not recognised by his teachers.

The information which I shall be presenting is based on the correspondence in my files and on the notes which I made at the time. I have changed the four names, but otherwise I have tried to record what happened as accurately as possible.

Case 1: Henry

Henry's father was a doctor, who wrote to me as follows:

> 'Our son aged 10 suffers from this disability [sc. dyslexia] though I have not been able to get anyone within the Educational Authority in which we live to accept him as a dyslexic and this is causing me considerable unhappiness and concern . . . Without an authoritative assessment of my son, it has proved extremely difficult for me to bring any influence to bear on the County Department of Education in terms of getting any recognition of a disability in my child. In fact it has been suggested to me that he is just educationally backward, though one assessment . . . left me wondering whether —— had any realisation of the occurrence of dyslexia, let alone any understanding of it.'

I first saw Henry when he was aged $10\frac{1}{2}$. I gave him some of the tests described in Chapter 2, and found him to be well above average in general reasoning power. I am hesitant to quote I.Q. figures since there are all kinds of pitfalls and possibilities of misunderstanding, but, for what it is worth, his I.Q. on the Terman test (see p. 46) came out at 123 (where average is 100 and only $2\frac{1}{2}$ per cent of the population are expected to score over 130). In contrast, when I gave him tests of reading and spelling his performance was approximately that of an 8-year-old. This discrepancy between intellectual level and performance at reading and spelling was clearly something which needed to be taken seriously.

I noticed regular confusion between b and d, although almost all children of normal ability grow out of such confusion by age 8 or thereabouts: he read 'big' for *dig* and started with a b-sound when given the word *dream* and a d-sound when given the word *biscuit*, while in a piece of written work 'bide' had been put for *died* and 'umber' for *under*. He himself spontaneously said, 'I sometimes get b and d back to front'. He also read 'was' instead of *saw* and wrote 'on' for *no*.

He had difficulty in repeating the polysyllabic words 'preliminary', 'anemone', and 'statistical'. He showed signs of losing his place in reciting the seven times table and omitted 'October' in reciting the months of the year. When given three digits and asked to say them backwards he failed on one of the two occasions. These are all items on which those with dyslexia have been found to experience difficulty.

The following are some samples of his spelling taken from school books:

Writing by a dyslexic boy aged 10

Electric fish

There are many strange and fascinating fish, but it seems difficult to believe that some fish are capable of generating their own electricity with which they can give a shock.

The best known of these fish live in warm seas. These fish have an organ behind each ear which is a mass of cells, rather like a honeycomb.

There Whears on anser to
this ecsept the noding of a
fyuw heads and the ciking
of the smallest sistes
a ganst the tadule. And
of curs it wars truw.
the chulgren war then and
poor and they never had
enuf to eat. The one father
had hide in a storm ov foue
years Be for

There was no answer to this except the nodding of a few heads and the kicking of the smallest sister's (foot) against the table. And of course it was true. The children were thin and poor and they never had enough to eat. Their own father had died in a storm a few years before.

As is apparent from these two examples a dyslexic child will often spell a word in several different ways on successive occasions; Henry's inconsistencies over 'fish' and 'few' are examples of this. Also, syllables may be omitted or put in the wrong order, as in 'elestricaty' for *electricity*. Sometimes losing the place takes the form of repeating a word or syllable, as in 'a a hone kome' in the first passage, and sometimes there seems to be no clear sense of where one word ends and another one begins, as in 'a ganst' for *against* and 'Be for' for *before*. It is these kinds of errors, as well as the b-d confusion, which often give the spelling of dyslexic children its bizarre character.

It is, however, highly intelligent spelling. Given that one cannot remember how a word is spelled, one can still sometimes *deduce* the correct spelling by sounding the parts of the word to oneself, and this is in fact what Henry appears

2

to have been doing. Even when the spelling is totally wrong, as in 'fyuw' for *few*, it is often possible to see the logic behind it; and from the phonetic point of view many of his attempts, even when wrong, are remarkably accurate.

I had no hesitation in confirming with Henry's parents that he was dyslexic. Later sections of this book will indicate in more detail what this implies. In brief, however, to describe someone as 'dyslexic' is to say that his difficulties are constitutional in origin, or, in other words, that there is some failure (though we do not know the details) in the mechanisms for perception and memory. This means that one cannot regard such things as poor teaching or parental anxiety as primary causal factors. It also means that the person has a disability – a definite *handicap* – which needs to be compensated for; and experience shows that special teaching is essential if he is to be helped.

The word 'dyslexia', when used of a boy such as Henry, seems to me to have three main functions: it classifies, it explains, and it invites to action. It classifies in that it distinguishes those who display this group of difficulties from those who do not, and the claim is that the difference is important; it explains in that it points out that the difficulties are constitutional in origin, and it invites to action in that, once a child has been classified as dyslexic, this implies the need for special teaching techniques.

The first thing, as far as Henry and his parents were concerned, was to give them a clear account of what the difficulties were. This I tried to do. Clearly it is no use offering remedies until one knows what is wrong. On the other hand it is a widely accepted maxim that diagnosis without treatment is unethical, and in Henry's neighbourhood there seemed to be no one who even knew about dyslexia, let alone had the necessary skills for teaching him. In this particular case we arranged that both Henry and his mother should come to me for a 'crash course' lasting a week and that his mother should take over the teaching from there. During this week I tried to show her the basic principles, as I understood them, that were needed for the teaching of any dyslexic child. One of the first requirements, of course, was to try to give Henry confidence; but this could not be done merely by telling him that he was an able boy. What was needed was to give him a taste of success; and I tried to show his mother how to move to progressively more difficult spelling tasks while making sure that each stage was properly learned before he went on to the next one. I shall not attempt to go into details here, but, briefly, the methods used were those described in earlier publications by Gill Cotterell and myself. Relatively few teaching programmes were available at the time, but Miss Cotterell's *Check List of Basic Sounds,* which forms part of her *Diagnosis in the Classroom* (Cotterell, 1970), remains a particularly useful guide. I do not wish to give the impression that parental coaching is the answer in *all* cases of dyslexia; some parents may not feel competent to make the attempt and in some cases other facilities may be available. It is, however, a possibility which should certainly be given serious consideration.

Case 2: John

I first saw John at the age of 15. One of the things which I was shown was a poem which he had written at the age of 10, for which he had been awarded a prize in a competition. I shall quote this poem in full – not as an illustration of his spelling (since the version which I saw had presumably been edited) but simply to indicate some of his feelings. The poem was entitled *What punishment is next?*, and it went as follows:

> I am tortured every day
> My hands or feet are blown away
> A rook's nest in my head, feathers in my shirt
> Handed down from farmers' wives.
> What punishment is next?
>
> I am lonely and the birds won't come near me
> Unless to take a grain of straw.

But me – I am hung on a frame
And cannot fight the evil world.

When gale force winds whistle past my ear –
That will be my dying day.
Me, a scarecrow, dead, nothing left.
No punishment is left.*

The following information was given to me by John's mother in a letter: 'John's first three years at school (local state) were very unhappy and he was placed in a backward class in the Junior School. He was behind with his reading but his biggest difficulty was his writing. After several abortive attempts to produce something that was suitably legible to gain his teachers' approval he almost gave up trying. The small amount of work he produced was mirror writing. He found it impossible to distinguish b from d, and some of his numbers were back to front [She drew a reversed 5 and a reversed 7]. Sometimes his answers were reversed, e.g. $5 \times 3 = 51$. We took him to see the educational psychologist and then subsequently were sent to see —— the psychiatrist . . . Briefly, he was an intelligent child with problems. We were advised to send him to a small private school. After an uphill struggle he managed to write but it was very illegible and dreadful spelling. Being able to write seemed to release a lot of tension and he began to write poetry. [He] returned to a state school at the age of thirteen years. He has learned to improvise ways to overcome some of his difficulties. He uses capital letters sometimes in preference to small letters because he does not have to worry about which way they face. Over the past two years he has tried very hard to improve the legibility of his handwriting with considerable success but his erratic spelling persists. Sometimes his words are quite correct but sometimes he will use two separate spellings for the same word in the one sentence, speak, speeck . . . Sometimes he will add extra letters, post, poast.

---

* I am grateful to the Editor of the *Dyslexia Review*, Mrs. V. W. Fisher, for permission to reprint this poem.

His creative writing is considered very good and he has a love of language, but we have been told that he will not get "O" level English if he does not master the basic skills, i.e. spelling, punctuation. It has been suggested he could do quite well at physics if he could write more straightforward notes . . . Although he is now a much happier child, I think sometimes at school he feels demoralised.'

She also sent a school report. Among other comments it contained the following:

'English:
A hardworking boy with a maturity of outlook and ideas but who cannot express these ideas in writing, which is un-disciplined with frequent misspellings and missing full stops. His handwriting also is badly formed.

'History:
A conscientious boy who finds difficulty in expressing him-self on paper. His writing is often illegible although verbally he is quite mature. Probably an average C.S.E. prospect.

'Spanish:
An excellent pupil in all but one respect – he finds difficulty in writing correct Spanish. However, there have been definite signs of improvement and I am quite confident that with encouragement he will overcome this weakness.

'Geography:
He gives the impression that he is hardworking but very often this is an illusion. He needs continual supervision of homework and classwork. It should be pointed out, how-ever, that he is always pleasant and helpful.

'French:
John is a hardworking boy, who copes well with oral French but he cannot transfer this knowledge correctly onto paper. In the examination his performance was poor due to this difficulty, and it would seem that his chances of passing "O" level next year will be marred.

'*Physics:*
Works hard. Exam result this time shows the definate [sic] improvement I have been hoping for.'

Before presenting my own findings, I should like to call attention to a number of points in the letter from John's mother and in his school report. I will begin with the former.

First, it seems that a highly intelligent boy had been placed in a backward class and was very unhappy there. Second, the discouragement was such that he 'almost gave up trying'. Third, the boy tended to do figures the wrong way round and to confuse b and d. Fourth, he had learned ways of compensating for his disability. Fifth, the same word might be spelled differently even in the same sentence. The difficulties reported here seemed to me clearly to be those of someone with dyslexia, and the early unhappiness is, regrettably, all too frequent.

I find it hard to comment fairly on the school report. No one, I am sure, could claim that there is anything really vicious or hostile in it, but I think one can fairly say that there is lack of imagination and lack of understanding. The 'maturity of outlook' reported by the English master is in interesting contrast with his 'frequent misspellings'; he is reported as 'conscientious' at history, 'always pleasant and helpful' in geography, and 'hardworking' at French and physics. Yet he is 'probably an average C.S.E. prospect' and the impression that he is hardworking is 'very often . . . an illusion'. Also his exam result in mathematics 'did not reflect his true ability' and his chances of passing 'O' level French will be 'marred' by his weakness at written work. I have known other dyslexic children who were in fact very bright but who, because of their difficulties, were reckoned by their teachers to be 'average'. If one reads between the lines, one can imagine the kind of struggle which John was having at school. The incongruities are plain: he is mature yet only an average C.S.E. prospect; he is good orally but cannot get things down on paper; he has the standards in

French and mathematics but cannot cope with traditional written examinations. Clearly he was right out of place in the 'backward class' at his first school, yet progress in academic courses is held back because of his difficulty in passing examinations. The pressures which our educational system brings to bear on a dyslexic child can sometimes, I am sure, be quite bewildering. Indeed it is perhaps surprising that most dyslexic children survive these pressures as well as they do.

John's mother told me that an earlier testing had given an I.Q. figure of 132, which is, of course, extremely high. I myself gave him a difficult reasoning test and he scored higher than the average specified for grammar school boys of his age, which scarcely squares with his being 'an average C.S.E. prospect', but when asked to read words out of context he was by no means free of error, and when given a standard spelling test he made an appreciable number of mistakes.

Some pages from his history book are reproduced on pp. 24–5. Elsewhere in his written work I noticed, among others, the following misspellings: 'marie on Twanet' for *Marie Antoinette* (later written as 'marie anne twanete'), 'woemen' for *women*, 'pniced' for *panicked* (later written as 'panniced'), 'indenoty' for *indemnity*, 'treay', for *treaty*, 'dission' for *decision*, and 'candediture' for *candidature*.

When asked to show his right hand he said, 'I have to think which one I write with', and when I asked which was *my* right hand (I was sitting opposite him), he turned round in his seat, saying 'Let's think' and finally came up with the correct answer. In explanation he said, 'I was going to that one [my left hand] as this is my right. But you are sitting opposite so I changed my mind.' When asked to say '5-7-4' backwards he said '4-5-7' and when asked to say '2-5-9' backwards he said '5-9-2'. He was, however, able to repeat various polysyllabic words, for example 'preliminary' and 'statistical', after me with no error. I gathered from his explanation that this was a skill which he had acquired through practice. His comment was: 'I do a lot of this in

Spanish; when two words are similar you've got to pick out the differences.'

His mother also reported that he had no sense of time: thus he might dress and say he was going along to the shops even though it was late in the evening or a Sunday afternoon.

3

later on however there was a complete reverse of
the situation when easten rumelia rebelled and
joined Bulgaria thus the (Anti) russian feeling
of easten rumelia spread into Bulgia thus russia
thoyht she could deal with them near a five but
rote both altogether thus she tried to seperate
them thus the other powers ~~isolated~~ (and) told
russia to leave the two powers alone the states
of Serbia, Hertzegovina, estern rumelia and
Bulgaria descided to join toghter to drive
as a united Bosnia (regues) Turkay out of
europe this thy ~~succeded in~~ doing but at the
trety of potmouth (verlydplin) it was shown
that the other powers had different ideas
as to how the states were split up this
(S) also (went to (slow) the increasing importance
of America in european History
* this codediture was known as the Loensoble
condiditure

I find it virtually impossible to read your
writing..

When I spoke to him informally I was fascinated by his
account of his difficulties. Here are some extracts from the
notes which I made at the time: 'If I am in a sombre mood
I write about infinity. They write about football . . . Just
my punctuation and spelling hold me back . . . I've suddenly started to spell Spanish properly . . . Sometimes when
I'm writing an exam – say composition in English – I have
to stop; it's like a mental block; it's for a few seconds. I
don't know what it is. It gets you annoyed. Possibly something to do with my subconscious – I'm checking the line
above.

'I used to have difficulty with reading and writing. Spelling difficulty didn't become apparent until I'd cleaned the
writing up. Mother was very good – she bought me some

books' [Q. Do you read for pleasure?] 'Some books maintain my interest – Lorenz on aggression – fish, ducks – I found it very interesting. I am interested in computers . . . Alistair Maclean, John Wyndham, *Coral Island* – I suddenly realised I'd read two hundred pages and that it wasn't particularly hard going. Reading comes more quickly than writing . . . sometimes I just wanted to go out and play golf . . . but will-power. I can write legibly now except when I am in a hurry. I am poor on punctuation but it's beginning to come . . . very few full stops – there's a lull and you put a full stop . . . I had to scrawl it down the best I could.

'I'm fascinated by physics. Also psychology – there was a fascinating programme on movement; do you need biology? I don't like cutting up animals . . . I can never remember 7×8 – mental block almost; I can do it when I think about it. The nine times I never bothered to learn. Just multiply by ten and take the number away . . . I've suddenly started to spell Spanish properly, not French.'

I have met few dyslexic children who were able to be so articulate about their difficulties. The basic facts were plain: he was an intelligent boy who had had special difficulty with reading and spelling; he had many of the associated signs of dyslexia, viz. bizarre spelling, b-d confusion, difficulty in tasks involving appreciation of left and right, difficulty in repeating digits reversed, and difficulty in remembering multiplication tables. As will be pointed out in Chapter 2, it is the occurrence of this cluster of difficulties which entitles one to say that a person is dyslexic, with all that this implies. The reported lack of sense of time seems undoubtedly to be part of the same picture. Spanish was probably easier for him to spell than French because of its phonetic regularity.

Because John lived at a distance and in any case was over the worst as regards reading and spelling I did not attempt to arrange any special tuition. I was able, however, to make a number of recommendations in a written report, including the suggestion that he should be given extra time in his examinations; this seemed to me particularly necessary in mathematics, where rechecking of computations was bound to take an extra long time. I indicated that his potential ability at mathematics might not show up if he was continually tied down with problems of computation, and that in many subjects, especially French, he would be likely to fare much better if he was examined orally. The examination system is plainly not geared, at present, to the needs of those such as John, and there is a strong case for pressing for appropriate changes. Meanwhile it was possible for me to discuss the situation with John and his parents and give suitable encouragement, while making clear that I appreciated his difficulties and his efforts to overcome them.

More recently, since these notes were originally written, John telephoned me to say that he had been offered a place at university. This seems to me to represent a remarkable triumph.

Case 3: Laura

Two years ago I received a letter from a speech therapist about a girl aged 15. It said 'I feel that Laura needs special-ised help . . . She is better at practical work than at academic and I am sure that her lack of ability to spell has hampered her progress in many respects, not the least being a severe lack of confidence when asked to write anything down . . . Attempts to provide a teacher who could help Laura on a tutorial basis have, so far, failed as there is a shortage in this area of suitable personnel.'

The speech therapist had in fact gone to enormous trouble to find help for Laura. Alas! It was a case of bureau-cracy at its worst – so much so that I was moved to make a record of the correspondence which had been written about Laura during the nineteen months before I saw her.

17th Sept. (Letter from neurologist to G.P.) 'There is no dyslexia. Mime is perfectly understood.'

29th Sept. (Letter from hospital speech therapist to Laura's mother) 'I . . . find she is of school age. I regret that I am unable to see her as the county speech therapist undertakes all such cases. May I suggest you refer her to ...'

Undated (Letter from County Medical Officer to Laura's mother): 'On making enquiries it has been found that Laura does not attend a L.E.A. school and therefore does not come within the provisions made by the ——shire Education Committee ... I was wondering whether it would be better to make arrangements with the Hospital Speech Therapist.'

28th Oct. (Letter from neurologist to speech therapist) 'I am a little bit annoyed about it' [the above letter].

12th Dec. (Psychologist's report) 'A very pleasant but anxious and tense girl . . . Laura's spelling is not a particular difficulty . . . Laura has been advised to write out her spelling mistakes very many times, so that she has a chance of substituting the motor movement for the visual appearance of the word.'

Jan. (*undated*) (Headmistress's report): 'She is below average ability . . . she appears brighter than she actually is and has never mastered the art of spelling.'

13th April (Letter from speech therapist to Laura's mother). 'We are still working at obtaining help for Laura with her reading etc. . . . I . . . hope you can be patient a little longer.'

19th May (Letter from Group Secretary to Laura's mother): 'I am sorry for the delay in starting Laura's tuition.'

Spring (No exact date). (From speech therapist's notes) 'The teacher employed by the hospital said she would undertake the duties, then changed her mind.'

Summer (as above). 'An excellent teacher who has retired was employed by the hospital (after much discussion in the —— office who said it was creating a precedent to employ a *teacher* for *treatment*). Dr. Y [the neurologist] backed me on every occasion.'

August (as above). 'Mother admitted for surgery . . . Disruption in the family caused teacher to be irritated by lack of communication. Teaching programme abandoned by teacher – much to mother's dismay.'

Autumn (as above). 'A deputy head teacher of good ability [was] employed by the hospital to teach Laura twice a week. This teacher was suddenly promoted to Acting Headmistress of another school and felt she could not undertake Laura's programme.'

15th Jan. (Letter from speech therapist to neurologist): 'A seemingly impossible series of incidents have prevented Laura from receiving treatment for dyslexia . . . I should like to suggest she be referred to Dr. X . . . '

11th Mar. (Letter from Dr. X's secretary to the neurologist) 'Dr. X has now retired from the N.H.S. . . . He is still in private practice.'

One week later I received the letter from the speech therapist from which I have quoted above. I learned then that Laura's mother was divorced and had recently needed some intensive surgical treatment. I also learned that Laura's headmistress had proposed to enter her for a C.S.E. secretarial course!

I find this a dramatic case in that it illustrates both human dedication and human failings. I was left with a feeling of deep gratitude that there were such people as the speech therapist, who had persevered in trying to arrange help for Laura despite all kinds of setbacks. I was also left with a feeling of dismay, not only at the workings of bureaucracy, but at the fact that well-intentioned people (as I am sure both the headmistress and the psychologist were) should get things so hopelessly wrong! To judge from the intelligence test results (see below) it was simply not true that Laura was 'below average ability'. She was dyslexic, however, and I can think of few more unsuitable jobs for a dyslexic girl than secretarial ones. The psychologist's failure to mention dyslexia, though not unexpected, was disappointing. The recommendation that corrected spellings should be written out many times was, I am almost sure, a useless one which would have resulted only in increasing frustration, while talk of 'substituting the motor movement for the visual appearance of the word' is, I suspect, pretentious nonsense.

My own testing showed Laura to be marginally above average in general reasoning ability, but she was below the 12-year level in reading and below the 11-year level in spelling. She had difficulty in responding correctly to questions such as 'Point to my right ear with your left hand,' in repeating polysyllabic words, in saying digits backwards, and in remembering arithmetical tables. Her mother reported that Laura had earlier had difficulty over b and d, and Laura herself said, 'It's spelling I find most difficult. I tend to spell some things back to front.' In her school books there were the following mistakes: 'hoildays', for *holidays*, 'solidrs' for *soldiers*, 'crital' for *critical*, 'strecaches' for *stretches*, 'amoinear' for *ammonia*, 'nessary' for *necessary*, and 'proect' for *protect*. Her teacher had reported that she 'will make mistakes which have been correctly written in previous exercises'.

Laura was not an easy person to teach, and because of distance she could come to Bangor only once a week; but, despite complications due to her mother's illnesses, she persevered with one of the Bangor teachers for over a year, and when finally she decided to stop coming she wrote an extremely appreciative letter.

Case 4: Robert

Robert came to see me at the age of 19. His mother had written as follows: 'Our local Child Guidance Clinic "did not believe in making a diagnosis of dyslexia", so, although he seemed a text book case, he never had an official diagnosis.

'He has done very well in overcoming his difficulty. He can read his text books, though he does not read for pleasure; and can write, though his spelling is still very uncertain. In spite of this he has four "O" levels (Physics, Chemistry, Maths and Technical Drawing) and is at present studying for three "A" level exams (Pure Maths, Applied

Maths, and Physics). The difficulty lies in his inability to take English "O" level . . . He needs either to get this exam or to get exemption from it on the grounds of his disability . . . I realise that it is much more difficult to make a firm assessment in the case of someone his age than for a boy of ten or eleven, but I think he presents an uncomplicated enough picture for the signs still to be clear.'

I was able, without hesitation, to confirm that Robert was dyslexic. His reading still showed inaccuracies; for example presented with 'siege' he said 'sage, no siege', and presented with 'pneumonia' he said 'phenomenal, no pneumonia'. Spelling mistakes were still common, and on one sheet I saw that he had actually misspelled his own name, writing 'Rbert' for *Robert* (this was not his actual name but the mistake was similar). He was able to indicate the right and left sides of my body as I sat opposite him but only after considerable effort. He said that when he drove a car he found the instructions 'turn right' and 'turn left' very baffling. He failed to repeat the polysyllabic words 'preliminary', 'anemone', and 'statistical' correctly and he lost his place in saying his seven-times table. I noticed that when I gave him particular test items he often had to ask for the instructions to be repeated, and his mother confirmed that people always 'had to say it over again' for him.

I had already met two relatives of Robert's, an uncle and cousin, both of whom were dyslexic, and Robert's mother told me that some other relatives were also affected. (More details about the incidence of dyslexia in this family are given in Chapter 4). The fact that other members of a family also have similar difficulties is, of course, itself confirmatory evidence of dyslexia in a particular case.

She also indicated the extent to which Robert had suffered earlier in life. I thought it would be interesting if she could supply me with further details, and a few weeks later she sent me a large amount of information, from which I have extracted the following: ' . . . You must realise that an open invitation to a parent to ramble on about her child is liable to produce several volumes of closely written waffle! I can only say that I *have* tried to pick out the significant bits...

'He was very slow in learning to talk and did not really start until he was two . . . He started school very happily and settled down well. The only outstanding feature I can remember at this time is that he would periodically get very frustrated at some communication failure. After a series of these he would get very upset and have a long fit of crying . . . After he had been at school for a bit I began to be concerned about his work. My brother had had difficulties in learning to read, and there were things about Robert which made me think he would have similar difficulties...

'I asked for an intelligence test so that we could have some sort of guide as to what progress it might be reasonable to expect. We did not want to worry if his slow progress was due to low intelligence. Of course, I was discouraged. "Once you get into the hands of psychologists," said the school doctor, "you never know what will happen." However, eventually two I.Q. tests were done. On the first . . . he scored an I.Q. of 120 and on the second 118.

'Shortly after this we moved and he changed schools. The new school was overfull and he was put straight into the junior section although he should really have had another term in the infants school. The school was streamed and he was soon transferred to the "C" stream. From then on we heard very little about what was happening at school. We sometimes heard stories about one of the other children, but never anything about the classroom work. We wanted to give him time to settle so refrained from being too inquisitive. He seemed to like the teacher, and she would respond to enquiries by saying that he was very helpful in class, that he was a co-operative child, and so on.

'His behaviour at home deteriorated. He presented a classic picture of an unhappy child. He would come home and start to tease the dog, upset his younger brother, complain that his older brother had hit him, moon around not knowing what to do, sit down to watch TV and almost at once find he couldn't have the chair or the programme he wanted . . . or something else would be wrong. During the holidays he was different. Of course there were still arguments, but these were of the ordinary sort which can be settled by the children themselves. They made camps in the garden, had a rope to swing on from one of the trees, and made all sorts of things from old grocery boxes. It took some days at the beginning of the holidays for him to shake off the effects of the school term, and, as the holiday drew towards its end he started to slip back out of his "holiday mood". As he got older it took longer and longer for the effects of school to wear off, and he started to anticipate the end of the holidays earlier and earlier. By the time he was ten the Christmas and Easter holidays were too short for recovery. It was the reappearance of his old happy self for a few weeks during the long Summer holidays when he was ten (a self we had not seen for a year) that finally decided us that drastic action was needed. We felt that even the summer break might be too short next year.

'Of course we had been trying to do something for some time before this. When it was clear he was making very little progress at school we had seen his teachers who had all been as helpful as possible. We had been to the local Child Guidance Clinic and had had a battery of tests and interviews. The Educational Psychologist had estimated his I.Q. at 108 saying that the earlier assessment was "an over optimistic forecast due to his age" but had agreed that his school work was far behind what he ought to be able to achieve. The psychologist said that he had done his best to find out if home circumstances, or my handling of him was causing his difficulties but had been unable to do so. He said that Robert was exceptionally introverted (something that anyone who saw him for more than a few minutes at this time could have seen) and that this was probably the cause of his difficulty. He would never be able to learn in the presence of other children.

'I disagreed. I thought the introversion was being caused

by the learning difficulties rather than the other way round, and hoped that he would improve if he could learn to read. I set about trying to teach him myself, keeping him at home on every excuse I could invent while doing some reading and writing with him. I did not officially tell the teacher what I was doing as I did not want to put her in a false position, but I think she knew. She was very helpful, and lent us books and cards he was using at school. We did manage to help him a bit in this way but it was an uphill struggle. The methods I was using were different to those used by the school (no good using the methods by which he had already failed to learn) and every time he went back for a few days he lost most of the ground he had gained. However, by ten he was able to struggle through fairly simple material.

'His difficulty extended to arithmetic. He couldn't remember the order of numbers, confusing 12 and 21. The signs were also mixed. To him $\times$ and $+$ looked the same. In a subtraction sum he could not remember which number he was taking from which, sometimes changing direction in the middle of a sum. Of course all these sums were marked wrong even though the actual calculations were right. This further confused him and he lost confidence in his skills at calculation. He thus got the idea that he was no good at maths and this conviction has taken years to grow out of. In fact I had always thought that he might be much better at maths than he thought. Many times when discussing a problem with his older brother, Robert would suddenly come out with the right answer, having seen the way to do the problem quickly . . . but the moment the problem was labelled "maths" he dried up again.

'We had cast round for something he could do which would be his "own thing". He took up shell collecting with the help of a very nice neighbour who helped him classify them. In time he got quite a large collection. When asked why he was interested he said he liked the feel of them, and demonstrated this by running his fingers over the smooth interior of a mussel.

'Feeling that the thing he needed above all was to be removed from the pressure of having to attend classes, we sent him to the one school in England where this is possible. We had already looked round the local schools and had visited the local —— school. But the doctor who examined children before admission said that he thought Robert had some sort of disease of the nerves (possibly chorea) and refused him admission. This will give some idea of the state he was in at that time.

'Once he was removed from the pressures associated with school he started to grow up. We had always known he was "young for his age". What we had not realised was that he had stopped developing emotionally shortly after starting school. Once he was free to grow he developed emotionally at the rate of about one year per term. It took him about three years to catch up with his chronological age.

'It was some years before he wanted to do anything about his reading and writing.

'At the new school he went to pottery and art classes . . . Finally he found out what interested him. He learned to play first the washboard, then drums and guitar in the school jazz band. He also showed an interest in electronics, and, one holiday, I read through a Tutor text book with him on the subject. He took the book back to school with him to work through again by himself. This was really the first attempt at reading he made although he had done little bits on his own before. Since then he has been prepared to read books about technical matters which interest him. (But still at nineteen years cannot read aloud from the newspaper with any confidence.)

'He retained his conviction that he would not be able to do maths until he had to accept the necessity for learning the subject in connection with his interest in electronics. He got through his "O" level in maths and then, much to my surprise, opted to study both pure and applied maths for "A" levels. He now says that he finds the subject enjoyable.

'I am convinced that, if we had not acted when we did to take him out of the school situation he might well have been in a mental hospital by now. He was getting more and more depressed, and was withdrawing from contact with the outside world into a world of his own. I think that if the outside pressures had continued for much longer he might have eventually withdrawn altogether.

'[In 1969 he] passed "O" level technical drawing but did a complete mirror image of one of the drawings asked for – a much more difficult task than the question required ... [In 1970 he] failed "O" level in English Language, re-sat, and failed again ... is about to sit "O" level advanced maths, and to re-sit English.'

In addition to confirming that Robert was dyslexic, I wrote a certificate which I hoped would be passed on to the appropriate examination boards. After the initial pre-amble I said: 'He is likely to be slow, because of his dis-ability, at reading examination questions and slow at checking calculations. He is "at risk" in that he may go "off the rails" with miscopying or misunderstanding unless he spends a disproportionate amount of time checking. The final result may therefore not be a reflection of his true ability.

'Could I recommend, therefore, (*a*) that he be given extra time, and (*b*) that examiners be alerted to the possibility of anomalous results, and that his scripts be considered in this light?'

Robert's first attempt at 'A' level resulted in passes at the lowest grade in both Pure and Applied Mathematics and a fail in Physics. In a letter which he wrote to me at the time he said that his tutor had noticed that in examinations he always chose the *shortest* questions, i.e. those which required less reading, rather than the *easiest* ones.

I still felt that Robert should be encouraged to go to university. When I wrote back, I said: 'It is annoying about the low grades, as obviously your *ability* is much more. But our experience here is that many people with dyslexia have persevered and passed exams even after quite a number of "fails" or low-grade passes.'

When I was approached by the University to which Robert had applied I wrote: 'I hope —— University will be able to accept him. I regard him as a very deserving case. Like many sufferers from dyslexia he has fought a real battle against the educational system, and this has called for both ability and determination.

'My suggestion would be that the Department concerned give him a thorough interview. He himself will be able to describe accurately his past difficulties and any residual effects which still exist. His spelling is still rather poor and he may take marginally longer than others in the actual mechanics of reading, though his quick intellect is an important compensation here. He is "at risk" in that it may take him longer to check that he has copied things correctly; if he rushes he might get circuit-diagrams the wrong way round, for instance. At an earlier stage simple computation was not easy for him . . . If the University is flexible in its examination system, he could be helped enormously e.g. by being given more time or in other ways. In a rigid conventional exam, where one is timed and has to check calculations, he is bound to be handicapped, and I don't doubt this explains his low "A" level grades, which probably represent the combined effect of high ability with slowness at reading, slowness at calculation, and slowness at getting things down. Presumably at university level one is glad to have mathematicians and is less concerned as to whether they are quick at calculation!

'In view of his ability I don't myself feel a university would be running any serious risk by accepting him, but I recommend a thorough interview, so that those who will be teaching him can be clear where his difficulties used to lie and will not be surprised if residual difficulties still show themselves.'

Happily, Robert was accepted by the University in question, and when he repeated his 'A' level examinations he obtained grades B, D, and D instead of the E, E, and Fail of his previous attempt. More recently he has achieved 2nd Class Honours.

There are a number of comments which I should like to make on this case. First, the degree of understanding which Robert's mother showed was quite unusual. I have met many families where something was already known about dyslexia, in particular an appreciation that 'something odd' is happening and that the child is not just being obstinate and difficult for no reason. In these cases one can 'fit the pieces together' for the parents, so that they can appreciate, for example, that problems over left and right and problems of memorising arithmetical tables are all part of the dyslexia. In the case of Robert's mother, however, there was very little that I could tell her which she did not know already; and it is perhaps ironic that she clearly knew more about dyslexia than the 'experts' at the child guidance clinic who were supposed to be advising her.

I have sometimes heard the sneer that 'dyslexia' is a label used by middle-class parents to obtain preferential treatment for less able children. Yet many parents have said to me, as Robert's mother did, 'We did not want to worry if his slow progress was due to low intelligence;' and I have met some dyslexic children whose parents did not know about dyslexia at all – and who could scarcely, therefore, be using the word for selfish or disreputable purposes! There have, of course, been parents who have been upset and distressed at their child's sufferings and as a result have had plenty to say; but it seems to me that if their child is dyslexic they have every right to take the matter seriously. To dismiss such people as over-fussy seems to me quite criminal.

Where a dyslexic child has been 'put off' reading and spelling, one helpful procedure is to encourage him with things that he can do well. Sometimes this is art, while in Robert's case it was pottery and playing the drum and the guitar. It is also very important to remember that those who are weak at calculation and remembering tables can none the less be very competent mathematicians.

Robert's story has a reasonably happy ending. One cannot but think, however, that a large amount of suffering could have been avoided had his teachers known something about dyslexia when he first went to school. In the next chapter I shall try to make some general statements as to how a dyslexic child, such as Robert, John, Henry or Laura, can be picked out.

2

Recognising Dyslexia

TO introduce the subject of recognising, or 'diagnosing', dyslexia it will be helpful, I think, to start by reconsidering some of the difficulties experienced by Henry, John, Laura and Robert.

None of them was stupid, yet in each case there were mistakes which were altogether surprising in view of their general intellectual ability. In all four cases there had been difficulties with reading and spelling which to varying extents had been overcome. All four still had problems, though not identical ones, over left and right, and all four were weak at various kinds of arithmetical computation. Henry, John and Laura all had difficulty in saying digits in reverse order (a test not given to Robert); Robert continually needed to have things repeated and is reported to have produced a complete mirror-image in a technical drawing test; John was said to have a very insecure sense of time, and so on.

In view of all this, it is perhaps helpful to regard dyslexia as a *family* of difficulties. Not every dyslexic sign is present in every case and similar mistakes may occasionally be made by those who are not dyslexic, but a person can be regarded as 'dyslexic' if a sufficient number of these signs occur together.

As has already been pointed out (p. 14), a dyslexic child can learn to compensate for some of his difficulties. This necessarily makes the problem of diagnosis more complicated. A particular child may succeed in a task where other dyslexic children have failed simply because he has been clever enough to devise a compensatory strategy. Thus

John surprised me by his ability to repeat such polysyllabic words as 'preliminary' and 'statistical', a task which almost all of those with dyslexia find difficult; but from his remarks it seemed likely that by looking at the syllables of Spanish words in detail he had somehow learned to study the parts of longer words in isolation. One cannot therefore infer that he had never had any potential limitation over repeating such words; it is possible that he had had this limitation and had learned to overcome it. What one meets on any particular occasion with a dyslexic child may sometimes be a sort of composite: he may have had all kinds of potential limitations, and one may be testing him at a stage when he has learned to overcome some of them and not others. To make things even more complicated, a non-dyslexic child may fail the same test item not because of any specific handicap but simply because it is too difficult for him.

By derivation 'dyslexia' means 'difficulty with language'; *dys* is the Greek root meaning 'difficulty with' and *lexis*, connected with the root *logos*, means something like 'language', 'speech', or 'diction'. Confusion has arisen, however, because people have associated it with the Latin word *lego*, meaning 'read', and have therefore assumed that 'dyslexia' means 'difficulty with reading'.

Derivations are not necessarily important, but this particular confusion has been unfortunate, since it has led people to suppose that if a child can read fairly well then he cannot be dyslexic. In point of fact reading for older dyslexic children and dyslexic adults is a relatively minor problem: most of them are likely to be *slow* readers – and indeed they are sometimes in a position where they have to choose between speed and accuracy – and there may often be a record of lateness in learning to read. More often, however, it is spelling which continues to present special difficulty; and the emphasis on poor reading diverts attention both from spelling difficulties and from the difficulties over arithmetic, space and time which have been mentioned above. Indeed, the substitution of 'reading difficulty' for 'dyslexia' results in misclassification, since there are many people who are poor readers without being dyslexic and many people who are dyslexic and yet are adequate readers.

There is no special mystique in picking out a dyslexic child. Although some Examining Boards and other authorities insist that an actual certificate of dyslexia should be signed by a suitably trained doctor or educational psychologist, the recognition itself seems to me to be well within the competence of the average parent or teacher, provided only that he or she knows what to look for. I shall therefore set out the relevant diagnostic signs in the hope that they will be of use or interest not only to doctors and educational psychologists in their professional work but also to parents, to teachers and to laymen in general who wish to know more about how a diagnosis of dyslexia is made.

In brief, a person is dyslexic provided (*a*) that there is a discrepancy between his intellectual level and his performance at reading or spelling and (*b*) that this discrepancy is accompanied by some of the supporting 'signs' which have been mentioned.

A word of warning is necessary at this point, however. One cannot expect a dyslexic child to make the same mistake on all occasions. For example, if you have been told that a child sometimes writes b for d in spelling or sometimes misreads b as d, you cannot be sure that he will make this kind of mistake when next tested. It seems more correct to say that the dyslexic child is vulnerable and therefore *liable* to make this kind of mistake even if he does not *always* do so. The same is true of other kinds of dyslexic mistakes. If he never makes any such mistakes he is not dyslexic; it is quite common, however, for a dyslexic child to misread or misspell a word on one occasion and not on another, or fail at a 'digits-reversed' test on, say, his first and third attempts but not on his second attempt. It is important, therefore, to look out for *inconsistencies* of performance and not be content with results when a task is given on one occasion only.

A necessary procedure at the start is to obtain an estimate

of the child's ability at reading and spelling. Various tests can be used for this purpose. In the case of reading there are, for example, the tests by Schonell, Daniels and Diack, and Neale, while Schonell and also Daniels and Diack have prepared tests of spelling (for details see Reference Section). If no such tests are available you may be able to obtain limited information by asking the child to read from a book that is to hand or to spell some words of your own choosing; but unless his performance is a long way outside normal limits it is hard by this means to be sure if there is any appreciable backwardness. The actual score on a standardised test will be a more accurate guide, though in addition to counting the number of right and wrong answers it is helpful to observe in detail the kinds of mistake which he makes, the time which he takes, his false starts and corrections, his hesitations, the amount of confidence which he shows, and so on.

His 'reading age' and 'spelling age', however, will be of help only if you know his actual age and something about his intelligence level. Indeed, this is an example of a general point which holds good for the diagnosis as a whole: *the meaning of a particular sign will depend on the context in which it occurs.* Thus, if you find – or are told – that he spelled 45 words correctly on the Schonell test and thus has a spelling age of 9.5, this means something different according to whether he is, for example, an average 7-year-old, a dull 11-year-old, or a bright 12-year-old. If he is only 7 and can already spell to this level, it would be fairly safe to exclude dyslexia then and there; if he is a dull 11-year-old, it is possible that you may find some dyslexic signs if you look for them; if he is a bright 12-year-old, then you can say at once that there is a discrepancy between intellectual level and performance at spelling, and this would lead you positively to *expect* further dyslexic signs. Even then, of course, it is important to be flexible and not to let your expectations affect the objectivity of your observations. If you conclude that the child is dyslexic, you are saying, in effect, that he has certain constitutional limitations; and if this is true, these limitations will show themselves in other ways, such as difficulty over putting things in sequence, difficulty in repeating digits reversed, etc. If no such 'supporting signs' occur, you will clearly need to think again.

Knowing something about the child's intelligence level is essential for accurate diagnosis. The whole question of intelligence and intelligence testing, however, is a controversial one. My personal view is that the notion of an 'I.Q.' ('intelligence quotient') has been over-rated and that placing people on a uni-dimensional scale in respect of the relative 'amount' that they possess of whatever-it-is is fundamentally misguided. Intelligence tests comprise a variety of different tasks, and adding up a person's successes in them is quite unlike measuring his height or taking his temperature. I myself, therefore, am opposed to thinking of the I.Q. as a 'measure' of the amount of intellectual ability which a person possesses. It may be interesting to see which particular reasoning tasks he finds easy or difficult and I do not dispute that there is justification on pragmatic grounds for setting a person such tasks. What I do object to is the assumption that one is thereby 'measuring' some uni-dimensional quality. There may be others, however, who would wish to read more into the notion of an I.Q. than I do.

If a child is suspected of being dyslexic the results of an intelligence test can be put to two main uses. In the first place, it may be possible to exclude dullness as the chief cause of his educational difficulties. Clearly if a child fails to repeat a long word correctly or has difficulty in saying three or four digits in reverse order, this does not *necessarily*, on its own, imply that he is dyslexic; in the absence of evidence to the contrary it might simply be that these tasks were too difficult for him. Such failures are positive signs of dyslexia only if general dullness has been excluded. I shall say more later about dull children who make dyslexic-type mistakes (see p. 63 seq.), and all that is needed here is to stress that their requirements are different from those of the typical dyslexic child whose intellectual level and spelling performance are discrepant. It is, of course, the mark of a skilled tester to find items which give the testee a chance to show unsuspected skills. In the second place, it is useful for a teacher to know the approximate level of a dyslexic child's ability so that he can work out what are realistic objectives as far as a teaching programme is concerned. This is a matter to which we shall return in Chapter 7.

If you know enough about what to expect from a typical child of a given age, then clearly you can form *some* estimate of his ability simply from listening to him talk. Thus if a 10-year-old tells you about transistors or a 12-year-old about the plot of King Lear, there would be a strong presumption from this evidence alone that neither is dull; but, as in the case of reading and spelling, standardised tests give you results upon which you can act with greater confidence. I am not saying that the I.Q. figure is a genuine measure of something whereas the result of listening to the child or giving him an improvised test is not; but the advantage of using tests from which I.Q. figures are derived is that these tests have been standardised.

Quite apart from general problems about the significance of I.Q. figures, there are special problems about ascribing such figures to those with dyslexia. In general, 'group' tests of intelligence, that is pencil and paper tests administered simultaneously to a group of children, are unsatisfactory. Even in so-called 'non-verbal' tests the child may still sometimes be required to read the instructions, while in 'verbal' tests, which necessarily call for the reading of written material, a dyslexic child may misread what is there or, if he tries to avoid this by being extra careful, may go very slowly; and in a timed test he will then end up with a score that does not genuinely reflect his ability. In any case there is not the chance in a group test to watch the child in detail and find out, for instance, which answers are difficult for him, why they are difficult, how he reacts to success and failure, and so on. When told that the child's I.Q. figure is so-and-so, you would be wise to ask what particular test was used, and if the figure is based on the result of a group test you should certainly treat it with caution.

The two most important intelligence tests which are given to children individually are the Wechsler Intelligence Scale for Children (usually abbreviated to W.I.S.C.) and the Stanford Binet (known also as the Terman-Merrill or as the Terman for short*). Details of these tests are given in the Reference Section. Even, however, if one of these two tests has been used, the difficulties in assessing the intelligence of a dyslexic child are not over. When the tests were published the needs of those with dyslexia do not appear to have been considered. Experience now suggests that there are some items which dyslexic children can do perfectly well and others which they regularly find difficult.

Let us take the W.I.S.C. first. This test is divided into two halves, known respectively as the 'verbal' and 'performance' halves. The verbal half contains a section termed 'Information', which includes such questions as 'Who discovered America?', a section called 'Comprehension', which includes such questions as, 'What should you do if you see a train approaching a broken railway line?', a test involving arithmetical calculation, a vocabulary test, a test in which the child has to say how two things are alike, for example 'cat' and 'mouse', and a memory test in which the child has to repeat a string of digits after they have been spoken by the tester, followed by a second section in which the digits have to be repeated in reverse order. The 'performance' half of the W.I.S.C. contains a section called 'Picture Completion', in which the child is given a picture incomplete in some way and has to say what is missing, a section called 'Picture Arrangement', in which cards have to be arranged in such a way that they tell a coherent story, a section called 'Block Design', in which the child uses blocks to copy the pattern presented on a card, a section called 'Object Assembly', in which the child has to make a representation of a horse, a

---

* Professors Terman and Merrill, of Stanford University, were responsible for adapting and modifying a set of tests originally devised by the French psychologist, Alfred Binet.

motor-car, etc. from component parts, and a section called 'Coding' in which the child has to attach the appropriate symbol, for example a dot or a line, to particular digits in accordance with rules given to him.

On the basis of research by Naidoo (1972, p.56; Reference Section) there are grounds for saying that dyslexic children find some of these sub-tests harder than others. I shall not attempt a detailed account of Mrs. Naidoo's procedure; but one of the things which she did in her research was to compare the performance of two groups of dyslexic children (they were classed as 'dyslexic' by carefully specified criteria) with the performance of two 'control' groups – children matched for age and social background with the dyslexic groups but not retarded in reading or spelling. The main findings can be roughly summarised as follows: the dyslexic children scored lower than the control children on the information and vocabulary sub-tests and appreciably lower on the arithmetic, digit span and coding sub-tests. In contrast there were fewer differences – and in some cases virtually none at all – on the comprehension, similarities, picture completion, picture arrangement and block design sub-tests.

From what we know of dyslexia most of these results are not surprising. As has already been indicated, tests involving memory for digits, as well as some arithmetical calculations, are regularly found to present difficulty to dyslexic children. In addition, in view of what many of them miss through lack of reading, it is not at all unexpected that they should score lower than the controls on the information sub-test. In contrast there is nothing in most of the items in the comprehension and picture completion sub-tests which would be specially likely to cause difficulty. In the case of the vocabularly sub-test it seems possible that two separate factors are at work: a dyslexic child's vocabulary may be wide because he is alert and has picked up the use of fairly sophisticated words in the home, yet it may be narrow because he has done far less reading than a non-dyslexic child of the same age. His score may therefore be a sort of composite, being determined in part by the kind of spoken vocabulary to which he has been exposed.

I know of no comparable evidence about the performance of dyslexic children on the Terman test, but I have found in my own experience that similar considerations apply. Thus most of them are likely to be successful with problems involving similarities and moderately successful on 'vocabulary'; but many are likely to have difficulty with tests involving arithmetical calculation and the majority can be expected to have difficulty over saying digits in reverse.

The conclusion seems inevitable: one cannot simply take I.Q. figures at their face-value. Certain types of failure, e.g. over 'digits reversed', can be regarded as positive indicators of dyslexia, whereas certain types of success, for instance in items which involve abstract reasoning, show what the child can do in areas not affected by his dyslexia. To add these two together to make a composite I.Q. figure scarcely seems helpful. Indeed it would be true to say that one can actually *make* the I.Q. figure high or low according to the tests used.

There is a further complication. If one presents an I.Q. figure, this implies that one knows what it means or what can be done with it. Now in the normal way the I.Q. figure is used as a prediction of likely scholastic attainment, and those who score highly are normally encouraged to do courses with an academic bias. If, therefore, one's purpose in presenting the I.Q. figure of a dyslexic child is to make predictions about future academic success, it immediately becomes plain that one is on unsafe ground, since, as we shall see more fully in Chapter 9, predicting what a dyslexic child will achieve academically is by no means easy; in particular much depends on the extent to which he has the opportunity to learn ways of compensating for his disability.

I am not, of course, saying that the Wechsler and Terman tests should never be used with dyslexic children. What I am attacking is the uncritical use of I.Q. figures. It is, of course, perfectly reasonable to use the test results as evidence for excluding general dullness. If an 11-year-old passes several items at the 'average adult' level on the Terman test one can rule out dullness with complete confidence. Similarly, if he performs at a level which is average for his age on the Wechsler similarities or picture completion tests, one can again exclude dullness. Indeed, evidence of any kind which indicates that he is capable of difficult reasoning tasks is highly relevant and it is this kind of evidence which one can hope to obtain from the use of traditional intelligence tests.

This, then, is the first stage in the diagnosis: it is necessary to find out whether there is a discrepancy between the child's intellectual level and his performance at spelling. If there is not, then one may conclude that he is not a serious or typical case of dyslexia.

In most cases reading as well as spelling will usually be weaker than would be expected from a child's intellectual level, but it is a mistake to rely too heavily on the child's reading age as a diagnostic sign, since some dyslexic children – particularly those lucky enough to have received skilled and intensive teaching – can read fairly well; in these cases the dyslexia may be masked by a good performance at reading. I have also met really bright children whose reading age is on a level with their actual age or even above it but who none the less are dyslexic. One is sure that they are dyslexic from the presence of many other dyslexic signs, and they are, of course, still 'discrepant' in the sense that their performance at reading, though not behind what is average for their age, is still behind what would be expected from their intelligence level. Such children are sometimes regarded as being average in ability by their teachers when in fact their average performance is a composite of extreme brightness coupled with dyslexia. Any educational survey which relies solely on scores on a reading test is likely to miss a number of children who are in fact dyslexic (cf. pp. 78 seq.).

Another thing to watch for is so-called 'bizarre' spelling. Plenty of examples appear in Chapter 1, for example Henry's 'elestricaty' for *electricity* and John's 'pniced' for *panicked* and 'marie on Twanet' for *Marie Antoinette.*

Sometimes parts of the word are left out; sometimes letters are put in the wrong order; sometimes there is intelligent but quite mistaken phonetic spelling, and sometimes several of these things happen in combination – in which case the effect is even more weird. This 'bizarre' spelling is easier to recognise than to describe, and from an examination of the child's school books – including those of an earlier stage if they are still available – the tester will normally have little difficulty in discovering if it is present.

The next stage in the diagnosis is to see if some of the accompanying dyslexic signs are present.

The first of these which I should like to mention is confusion between b and d. Once again one needs to bear in mind the age and intelligence of the child. Before the age of about 7½ such confusions can be regarded as possible warning signs, but cannot be regarded as decisive evidence of dyslexia. After the age of 8, however, few non-dyslexic children of average ability display these confusions; and it follows that if you are dealing with a bright 8- or 9-year-old who has other dyslexic signs, the presence of b-d confusion will be further confirmation that he is dyslexic. In the case of older children, that is those of 12 and upwards, it is possible that they themselves will not remember that they ever confused b and d, though I have sometimes discovered afterwards from talking to their parents that in fact they did so at an earlier age.

It is also important to check whether b-d confusion occurs in both reading and writing or whether it occurs in writing only. (I do not know of any cases where it has occurred in reading only, but this is not to say that no such cases exist.) If one is inspecting school books for bizarre spelling it is helpful to look out for b-d confusion at the same time.

The next stage in the diagnosis is to see if the child has a clear conception of left and right. It may be helpful, even in the case of older children and adults, to start with a simple request such as 'Show me your right hand'. Even here one occasionally finds surprising results – a significant pause or the invoking of a special mnemonic. In the case of more articulate children one may sometimes be told, 'I used to get very muddled' or even 'I've learned now – the *right* hand is the one I *write* with', or 'It's the hand with the scar [or ring] on', or 'I know my watch is on my left hand, so my right must be the other one'. A more difficult task is involved if, sitting opposite the child, you say, 'Which is *my* right hand?' or 'Point to my left ear with your right hand'. In recent months, however, I have become somewhat less confident about the value of such tests for picking out dyslexic children, since it is possible that the task is difficult for some non-dyslexic children too. If, therefore, there were few other positive signs in the rest of the assessment one would be wrong, I am sure, to attach too much importance to a failure on such tests. If, however, it is accompanied by other signs of dyslexia, one may reasonably regard such failure as additional evidence that the child is dyslexic.

Some years ago, after giving the Schonell reading test to a number of older dyslexic children, I happened to notice that most of them were stumbling over the word 'preliminary'. I have since noticed that various other longer words seem to cause difficulty, for example 'statistical', 'philosophical' and 'anemone' (often repeated as 'an enemy'). Some rough surveys have indicated that quite a large number of 9-year-olds may have difficulty in correctly repeating words of this complexity, but in a bright child of 10 or more it seems perfectly safe to regard such failure as a positive sign of dyslexia. This is confirmed by a study of the attempts which dyslexic children make at spelling 'preliminary': syllables are omitted and letters are confused in a most curious way. The following are examples from our Bangor records: 'plemerrley', 'premerriley', 'pellimery', 'preliary', 'plerminary', 'plemerly' and 'pliminary'.

When dyslexic children are asked to say these longer words there is often the same sequence of behaviour: they make an attempt which is somewhere near correct, and if you then ask them to repeat the word they say part of it and then hesitate and become confused. At this point they may smile in a sheepish way, sometimes with an indication of exasperation at their failure. It is as though both of you were acknowledging the incongruity – and perhaps even the humour – of this kind of failure.

It has been mentioned already that those with dyslexia seem to have special difficulty in saying digits in reverse order. To check on this I have found it helpful to adapt the procedure used in the Wechsler test: I tell the child that I will be saying some numbers and that he is to say them backwards, and he is then given an example for practice, such as, 'If I were to say 4-2-7, what would you say?' If he replies '7-2-4' then he has grasped what is required. The digits should be presented at the rate of about one per second. If the child has difficulty outside normal limits, this again is a positive indication of dyslexia. Experience is perhaps the main guide as to what are 'normal limits', but as a rough indication it is worth noting that the Terman test (which has been given to many thousands of children) puts 'four digits reversed' at age 9, 'five digits reversed' at age 12, and 'six digits reversed' at the first grade of 'superior adult'. As with many tests for dyslexia, however, interest lies less in correctness as such than in the way in which the child sets to work. I have met very few dyslexic children who have failed at three digits reversed on every trial, but I have met plenty who have failed at, say, two attempts out of three. Throughout the diagnosis one is trying to find whether the child is *vulnerable* at a particular task, not whether he can occasionally produce the right answer.

I have also found it useful to ask the child to say the months of the year. Some dyslexic children can do this task successfully, but quite a number either omit months or put them in the wrong order. Older children and adults can be asked to say the months of the year backwards, and it will soon be apparent if the person has any unusual difficulty. Once again correctness is not the main thing to watch for; a very bright dyslexic child may be able to bring in all sorts of compensatory devices as a result of which the correct answer emerges, but if, for instance, before answering he said them forwards under his breath, one would certainly be entitled to say that the condition of 'unusual difficulty' was satisfied.

Some dyslexic children have difficulty with numbers. They cannot, for instance, do subtraction unless they first represent the numbers in concrete form – by counting on their fingers, for instance, or by using marks on paper or beads or blocks. This, however, does not happen invariably.

What is far more common is difficulty in remembering and reciting arithmetical tables. This is one of the areas in which dyslexic children have continually been dubbed 'lazy', but the difficulty is so widespread that it cannot be accidental. Most of them can remember the obvious products, such as 2×3, and, where there is a clear rule, as in the case of the ten-times and eleven-times tables, they are able to apply it. What is difficult for them is to answer on the spot such questions as 'What is 6×7?' or 'What is 8×7?' (compare the report of the conversation with John, p. 26). In addition, if asked to recite tables in the traditional way, for example 'One six is six, two sixes are twelve', they are liable to lose their place, perhaps by passing from five sixes to seven sixes, or to hesitate and say 'Where have I got to?' This 'where-have-I-got-to?' response occurs fairly regularly even with older dyslexic children.

Some dyslexic children are reported as being unusually clumsy and some are said to have been late at walking and/or talking. Although these signs do not occur in every case, they are sufficiently frequent to be regarded as confirmatory evidence that the child is dyslexic, provided some of the main dyslexic signs are also present.

The following, then, are some of the main signs of dyslexia to look out for:
(i) discrepancy between intellectual level and performance at spelling, (ii) bizarre spelling, (iii) confusion of b and d in either reading or writing, or in both, (iv) difficulty over distinguishing left and right, (v) difficulty in repeating polysyllabic words such as 'preliminary', 'philosophical', 's'atistical', and 'anemone', (vi) difficulty in repeating digits

in reverse order (and other defects of short term memory), (vii) difficulty in repeating months of the year, especially in reverse order, (viii) inability to do subtractions except with 'concrete' aids, (ix) difficulty in memorising arithmetical tables, (x) 'losing the place' when reciting tables, (xi) a history of clumsiness, late walking, or late talking.

Not all these signs will be present in any one child, but if the discrepancy between intellectual level and performance at spelling is accompanied by four or more of them it is safe to say that the child is dyslexic; and this is, in effect, to say that his educational difficulties have a constitutional basis.

If possible, it is also helpful to try to discover if any other members of the family have had similiar difficulties. There are some occasions when the result may be negative, but if it is positive one's confidence that this particular child is dyslexic is very much increased. The question of the incidence of dyslexia in families will be discussed further in Chapter 4.

1987 Edition

pp. 46–49   With regard to my earlier comments on intelligence testing, evidence is now available about the performance of dyslexic children both on the W.I.S.C. and on the British Ability Scales (see Miles and Ellis, 1981; Thomson, 1982). The evidence cited in Chapter 10 suggests that any task calling for rapid processing of symbolic material is likely to cause difficulty to dyslexics of all ages; and it follows that if such tasks are included as part of an intelligence test the dyslexic's total score will be 'pulled down' and the resultant I.Q. figure will be too low.

pp. 50-54   The 'accompanying dyslexic signs' referred to in the second half of this chapter have now been studied in more detail. A system of scoring has been evolved (Miles, 1983) which takes account not only of whether the person responds correctly but of such things as special strategies, hesitations, earlier difficulty, requests for the question to be repeated, and the like. As a result it is possible to score each set of items (e.g. reciting tables, repeating digits, etc.) as 'plus' (= dyslexia-positive); if the person answers wrongly, needs a special strategy, etc., as 'minus (= dyslexia-negative); if the person shows no particular difficulty, or as 'zero' if there are slight hesitations etc. without <u>severe</u> difficulty. Many of the items referred to on pp.53 and 54 have been collected together to form the Bangor Dyslexia Test (Miles, 1982).

It was also possible to give these items to non-dyslexic children in a number of local schools. These children were matched as far as possible for both age and intelligence with children who had been assessed by me as dyslexic but with the important difference that, to be counted as 'non-dyslexic', every child had to score above a specified level on the Schonell spelling test. This was in effect a way of putting the Bangor Dyslexia test 'on trial', since if the items in it were of no special significance there would be no reason to expect any difference in score between the two groups. What emerged, in fact, was that the dyslexics consistently showed more 'pluses' (or 'dyslexia-positive' signs) on each item than did the controls. By way of illustration the following table, taken from Miles (1983) p.56, shows the percentage of 'pluses' for those dyslexic and control children who were between the ages of 9 and 12. There were 80 children in each group.

Test-item	Dyslexics	Controls
	(Percentage of 'pluses')	
Digits reversed	80	48
Left-right	78	42
Polysyllables	56	24
Subtraction	58	19
Tables	96	51
Months forwards	60	13
Months reversed	86	28

It is interesting to note from these figures that a 'minus' on tables appears to be a strong negative indicator and that a 'plus' on Months forwards appears to be a strong positive one. Perhaps more important, these figures lend support to the view that we *all* make dyslexic-type mistakes from time to time. In other words, it is not the case (as might have been supposed by someone unfamiliar with dyslexia) that dyslexics *always* make a certain kind of mistake and that non-dyslexics *never* do. It is rather that dyslexics are more vulnerable and make such mistakes more often. One can therefore say that one or two 'pluses' on their own are of no special significance but that it is the *accumulation* of small signs, *taken in conjunction,* which adds up to dyslexia.

The caution which I expressed on p.51 (where I indicated that I had become less confident over the diagnostic value of items such as 'Point to my right ear with your left hand') seems to have been unnecessary, since in fact 80% of the dyslexics in this age range scored 'plus' on this item compared with only 48% of the controls.

* These notes were prepared for the 1987 edition.

3
Doubtful Cases

THERE are plenty of cases where it is possible to say without hesitation that a child is dyslexic. Occasionally, however, I have been in the situation where I was unsure whether the child was genuinely dyslexic or not.

One can, of course, be doubtful about how to designate a child for a variety of reasons. For instance, if one needs data for research purposes an extra degree of caution is desirable simply as a safety measure; to include 'doubtful' cases in one's statistical tables is to run the risk of drawing faulty conclusions. There may be other situations, however, where the reason for doubt is not academic caution but a genuine uncertainty as to how a particular child can best be helped. In the case of a dyslexic child the basic requirement is specialist teaching, and while one can envisage few occasions where such a programme would do positive harm if the child turned out not to be dyslexic, there might be situations where it was irrelevant and therefore time-wasting. In particular, if resources are limited, one wants to be sure that specialist skills are going to those who need them most.

The semantic problems in this area are awkward. One is sometimes tempted to say, 'Provided people agree that the child needs help then the name given to his difficulties does not matter'. This, however, is unsatisfactory. Words serve to classify; and while it is unimportant which of two words is used if they are synonymous and therefore carry the same implications, there may be situations where the wrong use of a word results in a wrong classification, and here the consequences can be extremely serious. For example, the terms 'dyslexia', 'specific language disability', and 'word-blindness' are all approximately synonymous, and which of them we use is relatively unimportant. 'Dyslexia' and 'reading difficulty', however, are not synonymous: not all those who have difficulty in reading are dyslexic; some of those who are dyslexic can read quite well (even if reading did not come easily in the first place), and all have difficulties other than reading. To classify 'poor readers' together as a single group is to ignore these important differences.

Even if this point is recognised, however, the semantic problems are not over: doubts about whether a particular person is dyslexic are not always due to factual uncertainty. To quote a phrase used by the philosopher, Wittgenstein, in a different context: 'We do not know the boundaries because none have been drawn'. If we apply Wittgenstein's dictum to the notion of 'dyslexia' it becomes plain that there is uncertainty as to what precisely is to *count* as being dyslexic. If therefore, we choose to stipulate what are to be the correct criteria, we need to be clear as to the purpose of the classification which is being made. One may sometimes be quite sure of the relevant factors while still being unsure how best to describe them. Perhaps we should speak here of a 'semantic' uncertainty, as opposed to a 'factual' uncertainty. It is as though someone had a clear view of a flower in ordinary daylight but was still unsure whether its colour – which he could clearly see – was to count as, say, yellow or green.

There are four main types of situation where I have felt doubt as to whether or not someone should be called 'dyslexic'. (1) The first is the situation where such a person is virtually a non-reader and non-speller and where there is therefore no possibility of studying the kinds of mistakes which he makes. (2) The second is the situation where results on reading and spelling tests are somewhat below average, but where the other signs, such as difficulty over distinguishing left and right, difficulty in saying tables, and so on, are so mild as hardly to be outside normal limits. (3) The third is the situation where dyslexic-type mistakes such as b-d confusion are fairly frequent, but where there is no serious discrepancy between intellectual level and performance at reading and spelling. (4) The fourth is the situation where a child has some kind of similar learning 'block', for example in arithmetic, but has relatively less trouble with reading or spelling.

In the first two situations one simply needs more facts (which may or may not become available), while in the third and fourth one is involved in what is partly an issue of semantics, since in effect one has first to settle the general question of *when to call* a person 'dyslexic'. These semantic issues, however, are often extremely important, since if we decide to talk in a certain way we are thereby opting for a particular classification and hence for a particular policy. Each of these four situations will be considered in turn, with illustrations, where appropriate, based on individual case histories.

Case 5: Raymond

(1) A few years ago a man in his forties came to see me. He could write only a few letters and could not read any words apart from 'a', 'the', and a few others. An intelligence test showed him to be of average ability and there seemed to be no reason in his previous history (such as lack of opportunity or physical defect) why he had not learned to read and spell. He said that at school he had sat at the back of the class and kept clear of serious trouble. At the present time he was employed as a painter. To avoid having to read or write in public he had sometimes invented 'lost glasses' or a 'broken wrist', and though he could not write 'wet paint' he had been able to manage 'WET'. From what he told me it was impossible to say whether or not he was dyslexic. Indeed, if in general one knows only that a person cannot read or spell and very little else, there are insufficient grounds for either diagnosing or excluding dyslexia. When he came for special teaching, however, and started to write words such as 'big', 'bad', and 'dog', I found that he was regularly confusing b and d. This immediately created a

strong presumption that he was dyslexic, or in other words that his difficulties were due to a constitutional limitation (with presumably a physiological basis). This presumption will turn into a certainty if further dyslexic-type mistakes occur. No issue of semantics is involved here; at present I am unsure because I have insufficient evidence.

Case 6: Elspeth

Here is another case where, again, the evidence is incomplete.

Recently, a mother asked me to see her daughter, Elspeth, aged 6 years 2 months. I explained that I would be unable to say at such a young age whether or not Elspeth was dyslexic; but her mother, who was familiar with the relevant literature, thought that a definite disability was present and asked me to do what I could.

When given the Terman intelligence test Elspeth passed three items at the 8-year level, and in general her performance was above average for a 6-year-old. Her reading age came out as 6.4 and her spelling age as 6.2. At first glance, therefore, one might suppose that, since she was not behind her age-level at reading and spelling, there was no special cause for concern. Moreover the fact that she failed to point to my left and right sides as I sat opposite her and failed to repeat the words 'preliminary' and 'statistical' was not evidence for dyslexia since any 6-year-old would find such tasks difficult.

When I looked in detail, however, at what she could and could not do, I realised that her mother's fears were very far from being groundless. (In general, my experience is that when observant parents feel that there is something wrong or incongruous about a child's performance at reading and spelling they are more than likely to be right; and if one fails to take such feelings seriously one is not only being uncharitable but also running considerable risk of being mistaken.) Elspeth had in fact correctly spelled the straight-forward words from the Schonell test, 'can', 'hit', 'lid', and so on, but this result does not exclude the possibility of dyslexia, since the words in question are phonetically regular; and it seemed to me perfectly possible that with phonetically irregular words she would have far more difficulty. Similarly, just because she could read fourteen of the words in the Schonell word-recognition test it certainly did not follow that reading in general was going to be no problem. She in fact wrote 'gg' for 'egg' and 'ysy' for 'yes', which are unusual mistakes, to say the least. Also there seemed to be some evidence of a difficulty over sequencing: when asked to say the months of the year she showed considerable hesitation and finally said 'December, November, April, July'; and when asked to say the seasons of the year she said 'Winter, autumn, spring, autumn, winter'. Although she repeated the days of the week correctly forwards, when asked to say them backwards she said 'Saturday, Sunday, Friday', then, with long pauses, 'Thursday, Wednesday', and with even longer pauses 'Tuesday, Monday'. While one cannot say for certain that such responses are outside normal limits for a bright 6-year-old, the general 'feel' of the situation suggests that they are. Even where norms are available, as in the case of the digits reversed test, the conclusion is not clear cut. In this test Elspeth was successful on one out of three trials, which means, according to the Terman norms, that she just passes at the vii-year level. In other words, we have a minimal pass at year vii from a girl who passed several other items at year viii with ease. I readily allow that the evidence for her being dyslexic was inconclusive, but it was certainly not negligible. In my report, therefore, I suggested that her teachers should be on the look out for an *incongruous* performance and that at the very least she should be regarded as being 'at risk'.

This, then, is another case where there was insufficient information. At the time of writing I do not know whether in the next few years Elspeth is going to display the typical dyslexic difficulties. It is, of course, possible that if she is retested at, say, age nine, the teaching which she has received in the meantime will cause a few of her difficulties to be masked; but if she is genuinely dyslexic this means by definition that at least some of the signs described in Chapter 2 will be found. If none are present, it follows that one need not have regarded her as being at risk. If, however, there are still incongruities, at least in the things which she has not practised, then even if she has learned to read adequately it does not follow that she is not dyslexic, only that by hard effort she has in part learned to compensate for her disability. In Elspeth's case I am not sure if she is dyslexic because I do not know what difficulties she will be having in two or three years' time.

(2) One may also feel doubt in the situation where some of the typically dyslexic signs are present, for example difficulty in repeating polysyllabic words or in remembering arithmetical tables, but where one is unsure if this weakness is outside normal limits.

Case 7: James

James was referred to me at the age of $8\frac{3}{4}$. He came out as average on the Wechsler intelligence test; his 'reading age' on the Schonell word-recognition test was $7\frac{3}{4}$ and his 'spelling age' was three months lower. (These figures represent 89% and 86%, respectively, of his actual age.) He made two mistakes in six trials when asked to point to the left or right sides of my body as I sat opposite him; he failed to repeat a number of polysyllabic words, such as 'preliminary' and 'statistical'; he made one mistake in a subtraction test; he showed slight signs of 'losing his place' in reciting his four-times and five-times tables and I found 'on' written as 'no' in one of his school books.

His difficulty over left and right and his difficulty over the polysyllabic words were neither of them, in my judgement, outside normal limits, and the single mistake in the subtraction test is quite inconclusive. The confusion of 'on' and 'no' is unusual in an 8-year-old of average ability, and the difficulty with tables surprised me. That apart, however, there seemed very little on which to base a diagnosis of dyslexia, particularly since his performance in the reading and spelling tests was not all that far behind the average for his age. When I looked in detail at the sub-test scores on the Wechsler test, I found that the typical dyslexic patterning (cf. p. 47) was largely absent: although weak on the coding test, like many dyslexic children, he had a high score on digit span (which is extremely unusual in a dyslexic child) and low scores on comprehension and similarities (where almost all dyslexic children score relatively highly).

The correct conclusion, I think, is that James was not a typical case of dyslexia even though he showed a few dyslexic signs. It was in fact possible to arrange some special reading and spelling lessons for him in which he was taught words containing the letters 'oo', 'oi', 'igh' (for example 'soon', 'boil', 'might') and other words which 'go the same way'. His teacher indicated that he had less of a struggle than most of the typically dyslexic children whom she had taught.

I have met very few 'marginal' cases of this kind, and I am not sure whether there is a reasonably clear 'cut-off point' between those who are dyslexic and those who are not, or whether there are all degrees of handicap from 'zero' to 'very severe'. I think it possible that some of those who have an inherited constitutional weakness (and hence are, if you like, 'potentially' dyslexic) have learned to compensate so effectively that almost no signs remain. Such compensation, if it has occurred, would admittedly be difficult to distinguish from normal growth, but it seems to me not impossible that some children who appear as marginal cases are in fact children who were constitutionally at risk but who have learned to compensate. This, however, is somewhat speculative.

The fact that there is uncertainty over marginal cases does not, of course, mean that a dyslexic child and a non-dyslexic child are no different!

(3) A further set of problems is raised by the fact that

many children at special schools or in special remedial classes (so-called 'slow learning' children) sometimes show the same difficulties as the dyslexic child. In particular, confusions between b and d are common among such children, and it is likely that many would show the same difficulties as dyslexic children over reciting tables, saying months of the year, and similar tests. If these difficulties are the defining characteristic of dyslexia, must one not conclude that large numbers of slow-learning children are in fact dyslexic?

An important criterion commonly used in deciding whether or not a child is dyslexic is that of 'discrepancy'. One looks, in other words, to see if there is something *discrepant* about the child's performance, and in particular to see whether there is a difference between intellectual level on the one hand and performance at reading and spelling on the other.

In the case of children in special schools it is particularly important to check in the first place whether this 'discrepancy criterion' is or is not satisfied. The fact that a child does poorly in certain tests involving the use of language does not entitle one to conclude, *ipso facto*, that he 'has a low I.Q.'. In such cases some of the items from the performance half of the Wechsler test should certainly be given, for example the picture completion and block design tests. If an apparently slow child is somewhere near average on these tests and yet is considerably behind the standard for his age-level at reading or spelling, then the discrepancy criterion is satisfied, and, if other supporting signs are present, he would count as a genuine case of dyslexia.

There may, however, be other situations where the child's mistakes are 'dyslexic' in character (b-d confusion, etc.) but where there is no serious discrepancy. Here, I think, there are advantages in making the 'discrepancy criterion' a necessary condition for a diagnosis of dyslexia. Admittedly, for all we know, it may be that someone who confuses b and d is similar, physiologically, to someone else who confuses b and d. At present, however, we do not know enough about physiology for this point to be of practical relevance. What is important, it seems to me, is a classification based on educational needs. I am not, of course, in any way disputing the considerable educational needs of the slow learner; still less would I wish to be complacent in saying that these needs are adequately met in the present educational system. If provision is inadequate, however, this means only that authorities need to do better what they are doing already. In contrast, if a child is 'discrepant', his needs are quite different. 'Discrepant' children who display the dyslexic signs require for educational purposes to be classified as a special group, identifiable by a word which makes clear that they are *handicapped*. They will be thoroughly unhappy and out of place in a class for slow learning children, and in this case it is not that the educational system should try to do better what it is doing already, but that it should set out to do something different, that is recognise dyslexia as a special type of disability and make provision for it.

If one allows that discrepancy between intelligence level and performance at reading and spelling is a necessary condition for saying that a child is dyslexic, the question then arises as to how large the discrepancy needs to be. Here it seems to me that the only relevant considerations are pragmatic ones. One must ask, Is the discrepancy large enough to be taken seriously? If it is, then to that extent the child is different and needs special attention, and the word 'dyslexic' marks the difference.

On this showing the reasons for classifying a child as 'dyslexic' are social and educational rather than physiological. Whatever the exact nature of the underlying physiological failure, the important manifestations socially and educationally are difficulty with reading and difficulty with spelling. It is therefore convenient to separate out as a special group those children who, because of constitutional limitations, require individual help in these two areas. In particular they need to be distinguished from children who are slow at *all* school subjects but who learn to read and even spell without too much difficulty.

Where the discrepancy is not all that great it seems to

me perfectly reasonable to say of a child that he is 'very slightly dyslexic' or to say that one discovered a few signs of possible dyslexia which were not severe enough to be taken seriously. There are, of course, parallels in other fields: a person might have a very mild astigmatism, for example, which was insufficiently severe to justify the wearing of glasses. In general, just because a particular handicap or illness can sometimes be very mild it does not follow that in the severe cases nothing needs to be done.

Indeed, with dyslexic children it seems to me most important that any handicap which exists should not be played down. An unnecessary diagnosis of dyslexia is likely to do little damage, since the child merely receives some extra tuition which he did not really need, whereas there is clear evidence that failure to recognise that a child is dyslexic (and hence needs special tuition) can be very costly in terms of frustration and under-achievement. Large numbers of parents have reported to me that they have been fobbed off with the facile statement, 'Don't worry; he'll grow out of it' when they told the teacher that they suspected that something was wrong. Underestimating the degree of handicap seems to me a far more serious error than overestimating it.

(4) Finally there is the situation where there appears to be some kind of learning 'block' even though reading and spelling are not too seriously affected.

Case 8: Philip

Philip came to me at the age of 10 years 1 month. The Terman test showed him to be of average ability; his 'reading age' on the Schonell word-recognition test came out at 9 years 4 months (93% of his chronological age) and his 'spelling age' came out at exactly 9 years (90% of his chronological age). On its own this discrepancy would not be large enough to justify the claim that Philip was in any way unusual. He was referred, however, because of special problems with arithmetic. 'What I find particularly unusual at his age,' wrote Philip's headmaster, 'is that he . . . lacks appreciation of order in numbers. For instance, in simple multiplication involving 3 × 8, he is perfectly liable to put down the 2 in the units column and carry the 4 into the tens column. I have used an abacus and virtually every other method to indicate tens and units to him, but nevertheless mistakes still recur.'

Despite his relatively high score on the word-recognition and spelling tests, I discovered plenty of signs belonging in the 'dyslexia' family. When I asked him to say '3-4-1-7' after me he said '3-1-4-7', and when I gave him three digits to say in reverse order he failed to get the order correct in two trials out of three (with, of course, different digits on each trial). This response is well outside normal limits for a 10-year-old of average ability. There was continual confusion of b and d in his writing, for example 'boll' for *doll*, 'barsing' for *dancing* and 'binermite' for *dynamite*. There were also strange spelling mistakes of a typically 'dyslexic' kind: 'prepterion' for *preparation* (later 'prparlion'), 'torw brigde' for *Tower Bridge*, 'wroy' for *worry*, 'Amecar' for *America*, and 'libtgh' for *light*. He needed to use his fingers for simple calculation; he lost his place in saying his six-times and seven-times tables, and in trying to explain his arithmetical difficulties to me he said 'All double numbers – I sometimes put them the wrong way round'.

If one insists that no one can be classified as dyslexic unless there is an appreciable discrepancy between spelling attainment and intellectual level, one cannot logically apply the word 'dyslexic' to Philip. The difficulties and mistakes, however, belong so clearly to the dyslexia family that such a conclusion would be absurd. A whole host of dyslexic signs were so clearly present that I had no hesitation in classing him as dyslexic, though I expressed surprise to his mother that he had learned to spell so successfully. On practical grounds, of course, there was no doubt whatever that he needed specialist help on an individual basis.

From a consideration of Philip's case it follows that considerable caution is needed in interpreting the results of

5

large-scale surveys. If one has figures only for I.Q., reading age and spelling age, one cannot logically make any firm statement about the incidence or existence of dyslexia. Compared with James (see pp. 62 *seq.*) Philip was relatively less retarded at both reading and spelling; yet the other evidence points inescapably to dyslexia, whereas James seems, at most, a decidedly marginal case.

I have also heard of children who were reported to have a 'block' in handling numbers but to have no problem at all over reading or spelling. Although I have not examined any such children myself, I have no grounds for doubting the accuracy of such claims. There is no reason why there should not be variants within the dyslexic group of disabilities, just as there are variants in the form taken by an illness or in different species of insect or plant. We cannot expect nature to arrange things in completely tidy groups for us and she certainly does not do so! There is no reason, therefore, why there should not be handicaps which are like dyslexia in some ways and unlike it in others.

One final complication requires mention. I have occasionally met or heard of children who showed dyslexic signs in addition to having some reasonably clear-cut medical condition, such as autism (see Glossary) or minimal brain damage. In the case of autistic children who show dyslexic signs one cannot exclude the possibility that the difficulties with reading and spelling have put the child under such pressure that autism, or lack of contact with reality, has been the result; but it is clearly hard in many cases to isolate cause and effect or to be sure of the part played by contributory or 'predisposing' factors. In the case of minimal brain damage there are grounds for saying that the total picture is somewhat different from that of dyslexia. Although these children, like some dyslexic children, may have been late at walking and acquiring speech and may show signs of speech defects, clumsiness and poor motor control, unlike the dyslexic child they are weak at *abstract* reasoning and often show an inability to think except in very concrete terms. A brain-damaged 15-year-old whom I met some years ago was able to pick out hammer, nail and pliers from a miscellaneous group of objects as 'belonging together', and he then said to me, 'You put the nail in with the hammer and pull it out with the pliers,' but he had the utmost difficulty in coming up with the word 'carpentry'. More recently, when I asked a boy who had signs of minimal brain damage how 'wood' and 'coal' were alike, he insisted on telling me how they were different. The typical dyslexic child, however, can usually do this kind of test with little difficulty. Thus although the signs of minimal brain damage and the signs of dyslexia sometimes overlap, there seems to me to be a good case for keeping the two conditions separate.

I have tried in this chapter to show some of the reasons why in particular cases one may be unsure whether or not to call a person 'dyslexic'. Absence of factual information is one such reason, but there are in addition semantic problems, the answer to which depends on how one chooses to classify. Most of the dyslexic children whom I have seen have in fact been clear-cut cases, but it is not impossible that from time to time one will come across children who are only mildly or marginally dyslexic, as well as other children whose diagnosis is complicated by the presence of additional factors, such as general slowness, autism or brain damage.

1987 Edition

An interesting development, as far as 'marginal cases' are concerned, is the suggestion by Critchley and Critchley (1978) that there can be minor variants (or 'formes frustes') of dyslexia in families where some of the members are more seriously affected. Such individuals may not be grossly handicapped but signs of dyslexia can be seen if one looks for them.

I myself recently had the experience of assessing twin girls aged 10 years 3 months. It was not possible to obtain firm evidence as to whether they were monozygotic. Janet was believed to be dyslexic and I was asked whether for interest I would like to see Mary in addition. When my colleague, Alun Waddon, and I tested them we obtained the following scores:

C.A.	=	Chronological Age
R.A.	=	Reading Age
S.A.	=	Spelling Age
V.I.Q.	=	Verbal I.Q.
P.I.Q.	=	Performance I.Q.
F.S.I.Q.	=	Full Scale I.Q.
B.D.T.	=	Number of positive signs out of 10 on Bangor Dyslexia Test
V.D.	=	Average number of digits correctly picked out from an array of 7 exposed for eight tenths of a second.

	C.A.	R.A.	S.A.	VIQ	PIQ	FSIQ	BDT	Visual Digits
Janet:	10.3	10.6	10.5	131	100	118	8	4.43
Mary:	10.3	12.0	12.8	128	101	118	5	3.57

Spelling mistakes by Janet included 'methered' for *method*, 'rinoserus' for *rhinoceros*, 'prapella' for *propeller*, and 'hevean' for *heaven*. Mary's mistakes included 'discription' for *description*, 'mecanical' for *mechanical*, 'anaversery' for *anniversary*, and 'hidrolic' for *hydraulic*. Janet read *adamant* as 'abamant' but in the case of Mary there was no evidence of b-d confusion.

I was fully satisfied that Janet was dyslexic. Her reading and spelling scores were totally at variance with her results on the 'verbal' half of the W.I.S.C.; her spelling was bizarre; she confused 'b' and 'd', and there were a large number of positive indicators on the Bangor Dyslexia Test. But how does one characterise Mary? Her reading and spelling were adequate, and the spelling mistakes which she made were in no sense bizarre. Yet her responses to the left-right, digits forwards and digits reversed items of the Bangor Dyslexia Test were very much those of the dyslexic person, while her performance on the polysyllables, tables, and months reversed items were at the very least *suggestive* of dyslexia; and in addition, for what it is worth, she obtained a very low score when digits were presented to her visually. In view of her twin sister's dyslexia it seems inconceivable that these results were just coincidental. The correct description must surely be that she was showing a variant of dyslexia – a kind of 'masked' form which would have counted as dyslexia had she been significantly handicapped educationally.

4

What Causes Dyslexia?

IT seems to me to be established beyond reasonable doubt that the difficulties which have been described in Chapters 1 and 2 are constitutional in origin. This does not mean, of course, that environmental influences play no part at all. If a dyslexic child is lucky enough to receive appropriate teaching at an early age the ill-effects of his dyslexia can be minimised; and if his parents and his teachers are sympathetic and make clear that they understand his problems, he will be under much less strain. In that sense an adverse environment can contribute to the total difficulties, whereas a highly favourable one can lessen them; but this is not to say that the adverse environment is the main causal agency.

There are, of course, many kinds of handicap, for example lameness due to poliomyelitis, where sympathetic handling can play an important part but where the basic cause is constitutional. The same holds true in the case of dyslexia. Indeed, however much a dyslexic child has learned to compensate, it is still true that he has a constitutionally-caused handicap.

Once a handicap is present there may, of course, be all kinds of further causal chains which lead to different results in different cases. Thus a child who is potentially dyslexic may be under appreciably less difficulty if the language which he has to write is a phonetically regular one – Welsh, for instance, as compared with English or French. Again, some children react to their disability by becoming discouraged, while others show extra determination to succeed. Similarly pressures in the home and at school may contribute to the child's reactions in all kinds of ways. All such factors, however, must be regarded as secondary: the basic causal explanation lies in some kind of defect in the mechanisms for perceiving and remembering.

The details of this defect are not known, and the amateur neurological speculations of some psychologists and educationalists often seem to me to be rather unprofitable. In particular those who suppose that there can be 'faults' in the brain in much the same way as there are sometimes faults in an electrical system are guilty of oversimplification. In fact, if one part of the brain is damaged another part can sometimes take over some of the requisite functions, and even when a child or adult is known to have fairly gross brain damage, as in cases of aphasia (see Glossary), compensation is often possible. In discussions of causation, therefore, considerable caution is needed.

The circumstantial evidence for a constitutional factor, however, is extremely strong. There are four main types of consideration which are relevant here: (1) the fact that the condition runs in families, (2) the fact that it is more common in boys than in girls, (3) the fact that there is a similarity between the mistakes made by dyslexic children and those made by adult aphasic patients, and (4) the fact that there is no regular association between dyslexic difficulties and any particular environmental influence such as poor teaching.

In what follows I shall comment on these four points in turn.

1: *The condition runs in families*
That the condition runs in families cannot seriously be doubted. Research reports from a variety of sources have been summarised by Critchley (1970, pp. 80 *seq.*;), who asserts that 'We owe to genetics the most cogent single argument in support of the conception of a constitutional specific type of dyslexia identifiable among the miscellany of cases of poor readers.' He cites, for instance, the work of Hallgren in Scandinavia, who claimed that, of 276 cases, 88% had reading problems

in one or more relatives. Also, in twelve pairs of monozygotic twins (see Glossary) who were dyslexic he reported a finding of 100% 'concordance'; that is to say, in all cases *both* twins had the difficulties.

It is always possible in this area to raise doubts about the quality of the evidence. Not all investigators have used precisely the same criteria for determining if a child is dyslexic, and, quite apart from this, accurate evidence about other members of the family is not always easy to obtain: the information that 'Uncle Jack was never a very good speller', for instance, is scant evidence on which to base a genetic theory of dyslexia! Even if one has a few reservations of this kind, however, the general conclusion that the condition sometimes runs in families seems to me to be established beyond reasonable doubt.

Our experience at Bangor confirms this point. Time and time again we have found that more than one member of a family has been affected. For example, a father gave me a description of his own difficulties which clearly showed that they were dyslexic in character, while his three sons were all found, on testing, to have similar difficulties, albeit only mildly in the case of two of them. In another case a mother, who was a mathematics graduate, reported regular difficulty over distinguishing left and right and actually made an error when required to repeat three digits reversed, while her son, although extremely intelligent, showed all the typical dyslexic signs. On a number of occasions I have assessed two brothers both of whom were found to be dyslexic, and there have been times when I have told parents what problems to expect and they have immediately volunteered the information, 'I think I have had similar difficulties myself.'

Within my own experience perhaps the most striking example of familial incidence of dyslexia occurred in the case of Robert's relatives (cf. p. 32). Robert's uncle, a university physics lecturer, produced a record, dated 1938, showing how he had been assessed at a child guidance clinic and found to be severely behindhand at reading and spelling despite an outstandingly high result on an intelligence test.

Even now he cannot do simple subtraction without using his fingers as concrete aids and he is said strongly to dislike reading letters in manuscript! His son, Alex, Robert's cousin, who came to me at the age of $7\frac{1}{2}$, was found to have an I.Q. of 144 and all the same difficulties. When Alex and his parents recently visited the U.S.A. they met two second cousins, one aged 10, the other aged 8. The older was said to have had 'considerable difficulty with spelling and reading earlier, but is now reported to have overcome the problems', while the younger was still 'having considerable difficulty with spelling'. Alex's mother told me that the great grand-father of these boys (who was, of course, also the great grandfather of Robert and Alex) had translated works from Russian into English, but had been very unhappy at school 'because he had been unable to learn by rote'; this was con-firmed by Robert's mother. All four of this man's sons were reported to be poor spellers; one of them, so I was told, 'read very slowly because he made the tongue and lip movements of the words he was reading'. Some of the evidence here is admittedly second or third hand, but there is no reason to doubt its basic reliability, and I myself have detailed evidence of Alex, Alex's father and Robert. In the case of this family it is, in my opinion, impossible to doubt the familial incidence of a disability. Any other explanation of difficulties occurring so frequently in such an obviously able family (even when the members were on different sides of the Atlantic!) would commit one to belief in a truly remark-able string of coincidences.

2: *It is more common in boys than in girls*
The second line of evidence, which again suggests a con-stitutional factor, is that the condition is appreciably more common in boys than in girls. Here, too, Critchley (*op. cit.*, p. 91) has marshalled the evidence. On the basis of nineteen different surveys between 1927 and 1968 he reaches the conclusion that the incidence is four times as common in males than in females.

Again our experience at Bangor confirms this. When we

made a check some years ago we found that we had data on 185 established cases, of whom 145 were boys and 40 were girls. The ratio of boys to girls is thus about $3\frac{1}{2}$:1.

As it stands, this evidence does not, of course, decisively exclude the possibility that social factors rather than genetic factors are responsible for the difference. Thus it could be argued that girls mature earlier than boys or that for a variety of reasons parents are more ready to seek help for a boy than for a girl. It seems to me far more likely, however, that a genetic factor is involved, since, even if these other factors play a part, it is hard to see how, on their own, they could explain an imbalance of this magnitude.

3: *The mistakes are like those made by aphasic patients*
The similarity between the mistakes made by dyslexic children and those made by brain-damaged adults seems to me one which should certainly be taken seriously. It is hard to argue convincingly here, since the appeal is perhaps largely to the 'feel' of particular cases; one is saying in effect, 'This feels just like the kind of mistake which a brain-damaged adult would make.' But we know for certain that brain damage in adults can sometimes result in difficulty in appreciating spatial and temporal relationships; and since mistakes made by a dyslexic child have the same 'feel' (as in my experience they certainly do), it is surely correct to conclude that a constitutional factor is at work. One is right here, I think, to follow the lead of MacMeeken (1959, p.27) who says, 'There can be no doubt whatever that we are in touchwith a pattern of difficulty *aphasic* in type.'

Critchley, too (*op. cit.*, pp. 73–4), though suitably cautious, is in no doubt about the similarities. 'When spatial disabilities occur,' he writes, 'they recall those met with in adult patients with parietal lobe lesions, differing however in that they are manifesting themselves at an earlier age, and that they are less elaborate and less conspicuous. As in acquired parietal disease they are highly diverse in their nature.' He goes on to describe some of the things that can happen in particular cases: 'There may be a dimensional confusion so that elevation and plan are jumbled up in an odd manner. Even greater spatial defects may at times be shown when the dyslexic draws from memory a clock-face or a bicycle. Their efforts may be uncoordinated and even confused . . . The dyslexic child may mix up extra-corporeal spatial directions such as up and down, and more often still, left and right. Prepositions such as on, under, below, behind, beyond may be muddled. In attempting to write or to make arithmetical calculations, the child may set down the words and figures upon the paper in an irregular and even haphazard fashion. Figures and words are not placed under each other in correct alignment: the left-hand margins may be too narrow or too wide, and often they descend obliquely.' Later he refers to children who show difficulties on the temporal side, and cites the case of a child who said 'the day after yesterday . . . I mean the day before tomorrow', when he had meant to say 'the day after tomorrow' (*ibid.*, p. 82).

In the case of dyslexic children it is arguable that one should think in terms of failure of development rather than in terms of acquired injury. This is the hypothesis of 'maturational lag'. On this showing a dyslexic child is *late* in developing the mechanisms needed for spelling, left-right discrimination, and so on. It seems to me doubtful, however, if lateness is all that is involved. There are doubtless many adults who have achieved success despite their dyslexia; but, to judge from those with whom I have talked, it seems to me incorrect to say simply that they have 'grown out of' their dyslexia in the way in which a child who is late at walking may 'grow out of it' and walk quite normally later in life. That they have learned to live with their dyslexia is not in dispute, nor is it in dispute that they may have learned all kinds of ingenious ways of compensating for their difficulties or covering them up. My suspicion, however – based admittedly on only a small number of cases – is that there are some tasks, such as saying digits in reverse order or repeating the months of the year backwards, which even dyslexic adults still find difficult; and in that case one is wrong to think simply of late development, but one should think rather of a handicap which will continue to be present even though the person discovers or is taught ways of minimising its effects.

A further point which needs to be considered is that some dyslexic children show evidence of minimal brain dysfunction: they are reported as having been late at walking and talking and are sometimes found to have mild speech defects and to display clumsiness and poor motor control despite ability to reason in the abstract (cf. p.67). In these cases it is reasonable to suppose that the same failure – whatever its precise nature – accounts both for these 'soft neurological signs' and for the difficulties in reading, spelling and temporal and spatial orientation; and it is not impossible that they are due to a somewhat more diffuse group of faults than those which are present in the more 'pure' and less complicated types of dyslexia. In general it seems to me that in this area we must face the fact that the difficulties are somewhat varied; certainly up till the present no very clear sub-categories within the group of dyslexic children have emerged.

4: *Dyslexia is not regularly associated with any one feature in the environment*

No alternative hypothesis, involving environmental as opposed to constitutional factors, seems at all plausible. If emotional maladjustment were the main factor, this would not explain the occurrence of dyslexic difficulties in those children who were not emotionally maladjusted. If poor teaching were the main factor, one would expect dyslexia to occur among several children who had attended the same class, and this plainly does not happen. If parental pressure were the main factor, this would not explain the variety of reactions displayed by parents to their child's difficulties; still less would it explain why children who were subjected to such pressures always responded by failing in the same specific, limited areas.

Certainly if one *treats* the disability as constitutional, the reaction of both parents and children is that this makes sense. In many of the families whom I myself have seen there has been complete bewilderment over the child's difficulties; and when I have indicated some of the manifestations of dyslexia (such as difficulty over remembering tables and difficulty over spatial and temporal sequencing), the reaction has almost invariably been one of relief that at least an explanation is being offered which accounts both for the child's obvious ability and for his failure in certain areas. Evidence based on the study of parents' and children's reactions is admittedly not conclusive on its own, but when considered in conjunction with other evidence it strengthens one's belief that these dyslexic difficulties are constitutionally caused.

Some writers have called attention to an association between dyslexia and unusual patterns of handedness and eye-dominance. In particular they have pointed out that dyslexic children have a greater tendency to be 'cross-lateral', in the sense of being right-handed and left-eyed or left-handed and right-eyed. It has also been suggested that in some cases there is poorly developed cerebral dominance: in other words the child is neither clearly right-handed nor clearly left-handed.

It seems to me that speculations in this area should be treated with a certain amount of caution. To begin with, many researches have shown that plenty of those with dyslexia are straightforwardly right-handed and right-eyed; and although there is some evidence that cross-laterality is more common among dyslexic children than among non-dyslexic children, any suggestion of a direct causal relationship remains unproven. Also such a hypothesis would, at best, account only for those cases of dyslexia where there *was* cross-laterality, and one would be in the uncomfortable position of having to find a different explanation for dyslexia where there was *no* cross-laterality. In my experience cross-laterality is of no special use even as a diagnostic sign, since there are plenty of people who are cross-lateral without being dyslexic and plenty of people who are dyslexic without being cross-lateral. Even though there are grounds for saying that more dyslexic children have unusual handedness patterns and that more are cross-lateral than one would expect in the normal population, the significance of this association is very hard to interpret.

One final point about causation needs to be mentioned. There is perhaps a tendency in the case of dyslexia to over-estimate the importance of finding out what causes it.

There are many situations where knowledge of the cause provides the key for appropriate treatment. Most of the standard cases of what we call 'disease' are of this kind: one kills off the virus, remedies the vitamin deficiency, and so on. Dyslexia, however, is somewhat different. It is not something which one 'catches', like a skin infection; indeed it is perhaps misleading even to say that someone has 'got' dyslexia as one might say that he had 'got' measles. A more accurate formulation, I think, is to describe dyslexia not as a disease but as a 'disability' or 'handicap'.

From the treatment point of view it is important to appreciate that the cause is constitutional, since this entails that we cannot attribute the condition to such factors as parental neuroticism or poor teaching. The precise details, however, are not of major importance for the teacher. This is because one does not attempt to 'cure' dyslexia by rectifying whatever the constitutional fault may be; one tries to alleviate a handicap by appropriate teaching.

Similarly, while it may be of considerable theoretical interest if future research shows differences in E.E.G. records (see Glossary) between dyslexic children and controls, as far as the practical problems of the teacher are concerned such findings seem unlikely to be of any help. The question which needs to be asked of a teaching method is, Does it work? In general it seems to me more important, at least in our present state of knowledge, that time and effort should be spent on the discovery of improved teaching techniques than that time and effort should be spent on research into causation.

Perhaps one of the reasons why there has been argument and controversy over dyslexia is that it lies uncomfortably on the boundary between medicine and education; and indeed some of the polemics which I have read have seemed to me rather like petty disputes over 'ownership'. As I see the situation, dyslexia is a medical matter in its origin and an educational matter as regards treatment. Both medical and educational considerations are therefore important for its understanding, but it is a mistake to emphasise the one at the expense of the other.

1987 Edition

Chapter 4

Recent years have seen a growth of studies of possible anatomical bases for dyslexia.

Of particular interest is the work of Galaburda and his colleagues (for a brief summary see Galaburda, 1983). This work has involved post mortem examination of the brains of individuals known or believed to be dyslexic. Galaburda's suggestion is that at an early stage of development there may have been incomplete or faulty migration of cells to the left hemisphere of the brain: in layman's terms the brains of dyslexics may to varying degrees be 'wrongly wired up'. Now there is good evidence (based in particular on studies of those who have undergone brain injury) that in most people the left hemisphere of the brain contains mechanisms for the control of language; and Galaburda's suggestion therefore fully accords with the behavioural evidence that dyslexia involves a group of weaknesses in the ability to operate with words and other symbols. There has been an interesting further speculation (Geschwind, 1982) that because the left hemisphere of a dyslexic person is relatively weak the right hemisphere may grow to be extra strong; this would then explain the particular talents shown by some dyslexics in what are believed to be 'right hemisphere' tasks, in particular art, architecture, and engineering.

There has also been research into different forms of reading difficulty which have occurred as a result of acquired injury. For example it has been claimed that there is a syndrome (known as 'deep dyslexia') in which the patients (a) find it difficult to read regularly formed 'non-words' such as *nate* or *hobe*,(b) find 'function' words more difficult than 'content' words, for example *be* more difficult than *bee,* and (c) make so-called 'semantic' errors; that is, instead of the correct word they read another word in the same category, for example 'chemistry' for *physics* or 'crocus' for *tulip.* A very readable account of work in this field will be found in Ellis (1984). How far it throws light on 'developmental' dyslexia – i.e. the anomalies of language function described in this book – must at present remain an open question.

It has long been surmised that there is a relationship on the anatomical side between dyslexia and unusual patterns of handedness and eyedness. This, however, is an area where one still needs to be cautious, not least because some studies (including my own, see Miles, 1983) have found no such relationship. In view of the conflicting evidence there is no option but to await further developments.

It has also been suggested that there is an association between dyslexia and erratic eye-movements. Pavlidis (1981) has in fact claimed that such movements occur not only when the dyslexic person is reading but when he is asked to follow with his eyes a non-symbolic object such as a spot of light. Not everyone accepts Pavlidis' claim, however (see for instance, Stanley et al., 1983); and this too is an area where one must await the verdict of further research.

Finally, with regard to the genetic determination of dyslexia, it is perhaps worth recording that in 1981 I had the opportunity to examine yet another member of the family referred to on pp.74-75. Peter was a first cousin of Alex and Robert on his father's side. At the age of 10 years 2 months his I.Q. (based on an extrapolation from six selected items of the W.I.S.C.) was 132, his 'reading age' 11 years 0 months, and his 'spelling age' 8 years 11 months. On the left-right item from the Bangor Dyslexia Test he said, 'I was practising the piano. The teacher wanted me to play the right hand and I didn't know which was which, so she wrote on my hand "R" and "L". Asked to say his 6 x table he was correct up to 4 x 6 = 24 and then said, 'I can't do it'. At a second attempt he was correct up to 6 x 6, and hesitantly succeeded in working out 6 x 7 and 6 x 8. He then said, 'Six nines are forty (pause) five – where have I got to?' Asked if he could say the months of the year he said 'Yes, but not in order'. He started with an f-sound (as if to say 'February') and, after prompting with the word 'January', said, 'January, February, March, April, May, June, July, November, October, December (pause), February'. He took a long time to do the subtraction items and had to write the answers down; he made an error in repeating 5 digits and failed both trials of 4 digits reversed.

Peter's father said that he himself had dyslexic problems, though only of a mild kind. (He and Alex's father were brothers, Robert's mother being their sister). The mild variants of dyslexia are what Critchley and Critchley (1978) call 'formes frustes' (see addenda to Chapter 3). In this particular family it is clear that some members are more severely affected than others. The above evidence makes clear that Peter did, indeed, have the problem; and the fact that his reading was adequate and his spelling not *grossly* retarded (perhaps because his high ability had enabled him to compensate) is no reason for underestimating his difficulties.

5

Problems of Screening

THE magnitude of the dyslexia problem is still far from clear. As shown in Chapters 2 and 3, there is no difficulty in picking out the obvious cases; but there may be children whose handicap is only marginal and perhaps others who, because of their constitutional make-up, were at risk but have learned to cope more or less adequately. Any attempt to specify what percentage of the school population is dyslexic will of necessity involve a somewhat arbitrary cut-off point. What seems to me important is a screening system which picks out those whose need is greatest.

In most areas at the present time the discovery of dyslexic children seems often to be left to individual initiative. Sometimes this initiative may come from a medical officer, sometimes from a psychologist, sometimes from a teacher, sometimes from a parent. It is true that in many counties reading tests are carried out on all children aged 7 and upwards. The objection to this procedure, however, is that it will necessarily reveal only an amorphous mass of poor readers of all kinds. Although this group may well contain children who are dyslexic, many of the brighter dyslexic children may escape this particular net, since their reading may not be all that far behind the norm for their age, their relative weakness being masked by their high intelligence. Such children may, of course, be very unhappy in school if suitable provision is not made for them.

I have come across situations where there is a serious failure of communication between medical and educational authorities. Indeed on one occasion I received a request from a medical authority (not in my own area, be it said) to assess a boy who might be dyslexic – only to have this request countermanded by someone who worked for the same authority on the educational side! Adequate liaison seems essential; and in a particular case it may be necessary to exclude the presence of handicaps which are primarily of medical concern, such as poor eyesight, poor hearing and minimal brain damage, before the correct educational measures can start. As we have seen (p. 77), dyslexia is not a problem for doctors only, nor for teachers only – it is a problem for both.

One possibility* is that every 9-year-old should be given a piece of free composition. It is fair to assume that those who manage adequately have no particular spelling problem, while those who do not can be investigated further. This, however, is only a beginning. One has to consider the whole pattern of symptoms, as described in Chapter 2. Teachers' reports may be very useful, and one possible procedure is to ask the teacher to consider the various items given in Appendix I (pp.145–149) and see if they apply to a particular child. It is unfortunate when large-scale and expensive surveys are conducted in such a way that they do not distinguish dyslexic children from other children whose needs are quite different. As we have seen already in the cases of James and Philip (pp. 62 and 66), two children whose degree of retardation is the same if one judges by the results of intelligence and attainment tests may in fact have needs which are entirely different.

The fact that things are at present often left to individual initiative is particularly regrettable in that large numbers of children do not receive the help that they need. A further unfortunate result is that, because the initiative is often taken by the parents, some people have been- disposed to sneer that dyslexia is a 'disease of the middle classes'. This remark seems to me both uninformed and uncharitable. Dyslexia should in any case be recognised not as a disease but rather as a handicap (cf. p. 80); and my experience

---

* I owe this suggestion to Miss G. C. Cotterell, Remedial Advisory Teacher to the Suffolk School Psychological Service.

in the North Wales area leaves me in no doubt at all that this handicap can occur in children of all kinds of social background. Admittedly it is the parents with a special concern for education who are most likely to take the initiative in pressing that something be done; and indeed in this book I have for the most part quoted evidence based on discussions with the more articulate parents. To suppose, however, that dyslexia is limited to the children of such parents is palpably absurd. The correct procedure, it seems to me, is not to indulge in sneers about the middle classes (who in any case are not the only section of the population to care about literacy), but to make methods of screening more effective and thus ensure that no dyslexic child is overlooked whatever his background.

1987 Edition

Chapter 5

The suggestion quoted on p.85, viz. that dyslexia is a 'disease of the middle classes', was never intended, as far as I know, as a serious hypothesis. The implication was rather that more middle-class than working-class children would be *called* dyslexic because of a tendency on the part of middle-class parents to use a seemingly respectable label. For what it is worth, however, there is evidence from the survey cited in Chapter 10, section (ii), that dyslexia – as defined in this survey – is approximately evenly divided between classes. Supporting statistics are likely to be published in the near future.

6

Dyslexia and Morale

DYSLEXIC children react to their disability in a variety of different ways. I have met a few who were somewhat happy-go-lucky, or at least managed to seem so, but the majority, in my experience, have undergone appreciable hardship, particularly if they had been at school for a number of years before their disability was recognised and explained to them.

It does not take long, I believe, for an intelligent dyslexic child in his early days at school to realise that he is different from his classmates. He may not know exactly what is wrong, but almost every lesson is likely to show up the differences. Even at a young age he may discover that other children can please the teacher by making the right noise when shown a piece of paper or a blackboard with what is to him a blur of complex marks on it, and can please her again by writing the right letters in the right order when asked to spell something. He may indeed discover that if these marks on paper are accompanied by a picture (as happens in most books designed for young children) he can gain some approval by describing the picture and ignoring the marks themselves, although his classmates, it seems, can say the correct words even when no picture is present. As a result of his failure he may be branded as 'lazy' or 'stupid', and may indeed come to believe this. It therefore seems to me particularly important that as soon as his dyslexia is recognised the precise nature of his difficulties should be explained to him. To pretend that they do not exist is likely only to increase his fears and uncertainties.

The fact that a child has failed in particular areas may

result in some cases in a more general sense of failure. Because he is no good at certain reading and spelling tasks it is easy for him to assume that he is no good at anything. If he has a clear understanding of where his special weaknesses lie, however, he will be able to make a clear distinction between these weaknesses and other things which he can do perfectly well. Above all, if he has regular experience of success in some areas, his difficulties in other areas will be less of a worry to him.

There is no need for him to become frightened of words as such. He is capable of deriving real enjoyment if stories or poetry are read to him, and there is no reason why he should not enjoy riddles, puns, and language-dependant jokes when given orally, even though it may be too difficult for him to understand what is involved if he is dependent on books and magazines.

Several people have suggested (rightly, in my opinion) that dyslexic children are often young for their age. It follows from this that a certain amount of extra 'mothering' may be very helpful to them; and it is a pity that some popular magazines and even, perhaps, some professional counsellors have tended to foster a climate of opinion in which the 'over-fussy' mother is adversely criticised.

Here, by way of illustration, is a brief sketch of a dyslexic boy whose mother had the courage to back her own judgement against that of her many advisers.

Case 9: Michael

Michael first came to me at the age of $8\frac{1}{2}$. His mother, who was separated from her husband, had been left to care both for Michael and for his elder sister who was also dyslexic. Well-wishers had told her that the absence of a father was responsible for her children's educational difficulties – an attitude no less cruel for being predictable. Michael was reported as being in the very superior range of intelligence, but when I tested his reading and spelling I found he had a 'reading age' of $5\frac{3}{4}$ and a 'spelling age' of 6½. He wrote *doll* as 'boll' and *cap* as 'caq'; *land* was written as 'lad' and *cold* as 'cod'. When asked to say the months of the year he replied 'I don't know'. and, after prompting, said 'February, August, December, November'. Then, after correctly repeating his four-times table as far as $7 \times 4 = 28$, he said 'Where have I got to? I get mixed up.'

After some abortive attempts to find a suitable school, his mother gave up the struggle and kept him at home, doing the teaching herself. I had given her some guidance as to the kind of thing needed with a dyslexic child; and I became convinced – as she was – that to place a bright and sensitive dyslexic boy in the kind of day-school which existed near her home was to put him in an impossible situation. Her well-wishers told her how stupid and over-protective she was being, but she ignored their advice.

When I retested Michael eighteen months later his 'reading age' had gone up by 2 years and 5 months and even his 'spelling age' (on a test which is unsuitable and difficult for dyslexic children), had gone up by 1 year and 4 months. At this stage, at the age of 10, he was becoming ready to go to an ordinary school. Fortunately a suitable one has been found where dyslexia is recognised and where there is a happy 'family' atmosphere. I myself believe that his mother was entirely right to have kept him at home in the meantime.

In general it may often be the case that the parents of a dyslexic child are sensitive to his needs in a way that outsiders cannot be. Adverse criticisms, whether spoken or implied, of parental 'over-fussiness' may sometimes be quite misguided.

Finally, it is important to remember the pressures which are imposed on the dyslexic child by the educational system. There is a premium on literacy, and in most schools most of the time there is, rightly or wrongly, an atmosphere of competitiveness. If a dyslexic child is judged by normal standards of 'success' and 'failure', he is bound to feel insecure, inadequate, incompetent. What is required is an adjustment of standards so that teachers will take account of what he can and cannot easily do. Expecting nothing of a dyslexic child violates his self-respect as much as expecting everything of him. What is necessary is that all who come into contact with him should be aware both of his strengths and of his limitations.

1987 Edition

Chapter 6

The importance of morale factors has very much come to the fore in recent years. The important point seems to be that because of his handicap the dyslexic may fail to notice points which to the rest of us are obvious. If he has not learned that '1415' means the same as 'a quarter past two' and that this refers to a particular time of day he may suffer agonies at the bus stop not knowing when his bus is due – and being too shy to ask! His uncertainty over time may lead to mistakes over appointments, with resultant reprimands for his lack of consideration and courtesy; and if he fails to bring his football boots on a Wednesday this could be because his knowledge of 'days of the week' is insecure and that the question of whether it is Wednesday or some other day has never had any significance for him.* If he does not notice certain nuances in someone's tone of voice he may not appreciate that a question is being asked – and may then be thought rude for not answering it! If he is sent to do some shopping it is possible, as a result of his difficulties in immediate memory, that he may come back having forgotten half the things that he was supposed to buy, or, perhaps worse, having bought entirely the wrong things. I was recently told by a dyslexic adult that he had had to stop playing darts because his slowness in doing the necessary arithmetical calculations was too much of an embarrassment. Another dyslexic adult was unhappy because he tended to 'go blank' if he had to write a cheque under the 'eagle eye' (as it seemed) of a threatening shop assistant.

* I owe this example to Mrs. Joy Pollock, of the Helen Arkell Dyslexia Centre.

In recent years when I myself have been assessing dyslexic children I have found that the really important part of the assessment is the discussion at the end when the parents and child are present together. Here we can discuss problems such as those just mentioned and explain possible ways of forestalling them. I often make clear to parents that, once the overall picture of the dyslexia is clear, a large amount can be achieved by straight common sense. For example, the child's school work needs to be suitably paced so that he goes neither too fast nor too slowly; effort should be praised liberally, and safeguards should be devised so that social mishaps such as forgotten messages and missed appointments are avoided. Above all the child needs an accurate account of the things which he can do well and of the things which he is likely to find more difficult; in particular it is my experience that many dyslexics need *constant* reassurance that they are not just 'thick' or stupid. It may also be helpful if the family can learn to laugh at some of the mishaps; thus 'You silly idiot! You've gone and muddled up left and right again!' is basically a sympathetic remark because it conveys tolerance and understanding. I have also found it useful to give what may be called a 'prophylactic warning': for example I might say to the child, 'You may still meet people who don't quite understand your difficulties and if they tell you that you are lazy or stupid don't worry too much; we know you are *not* stupid' ('we' referring to myself and the parents).

The following check-list may be of help to those professional workers (doctors, psychologists, teachers, health visitors, etc.) who are involved in testing or counselling dyslexic children:*

1. Was it made clear to the child at the start that he is not 'on trial' but that what is being done is aimed at *helping* him?

2. How much was said about the child's *strong* points?

3. Did you make clear that you sympathised with the parents in their struggles to get help? Was any attempt made to remove the impression which they could have been given in the past that they were 'over-fussy'?

4. Was anything said about social problems such as forgotten messages?

5. Was the issue of the child's intelligence discussed? Was the question faced that both the child and others may have underestimated his potential?

6. Were the parents asked if the diagnosis made sense?

7. Was the child asked this?

8. Was a prophylactic warning given?

9. Was anything said about the extra comforting and reassurance needed by the dyslexic child?

This list is not intended to be exhaustive, but reference to it may suggest to professionals possible ways of making their counselling more effective.

---

* I am grateful to my friend and colleague, Pauline Brain, for her assistance in drawing up this list.

7

Organising the Teaching

IT is not the purpose of this chapter to offer a detailed training programme for dyslexic pupils. This is a specialist matter which cannot be dealt with in a few pages, and those who wish for further information are referred to the teaching programmes described in Appendix II. My intention in what follows is to help administrators, parents, head teachers, class teachers and others to check that appropriate procedures are being followed.

I shall begin (1) by making some suggestions on how best to find the right teacher; next (2) I shall comment on the timing and venue of lessons; after that (3) I shall talk about possible targets to be achieved, and finally (4) I shall try to indicate what are the essential features of any teaching scheme which is intended primarily for dyslexic pupils.

(1) At the time of writing (though this may not hold in the future) one cannot, I think, be over-particular as to whether the proposed teacher has the appropriate paper qualifications. A willingness to understand the child's difficulties is far more important.

I have occasionally met qualified teachers who give the impression that they think they 'know all the answers'. They report that they have never failed to teach a child to read (which may in fact be true, though I cannot believe that it is true in the case of teaching to spell), and if they believe in dyslexia at all one gets the impression that they do not understand what it involves. From the nature of the case such a teacher will not be able to show appropriate sympathy.

To take the child's dyslexia seriously is to recognise that he has a disability or handicap. Such recognition is perfectly possible for those who have had little or no teaching experience. If the person is flexible in his approach, willing to learn, and willing to profit from his mistakes, he may well be more effective than those who on paper are better qualified. By 'he' I mean, of course, 'he or she', for many successful teachers of dyslexic children have in fact been women. Whether to opt for a man or woman teacher will depend on the circumstances of each case. I have met many children who were ready and willing to learn from either.

Despite the flexibility which is needed, I have not found age to be a serious obstacle. Those who have retired from full-time active teaching or work at colleges of education may often be glad to do part-time work with dyslexic children, and I have known several cases where such people have been extremely successful. In the case of older and more intelligent dyslexic children it is perhaps desirable that the teacher should be a graduate or at least someone who can provide suitable intellectual stimulation.

In some cases considerable help can be given by the child's parents. As I have indicated already (p. 88), it seems to me important that one should forget some of the things which one reads in the press and in educational books about 'problem parents'. I have met a number of families where the mother has successfully embarked on a remedial programme, as happened in the cases of Henry (p. 15 seq.) and Michael (pp. 88-90), and on one occasion the teaching was done by the father. Clearly the position will vary from one family to another, but in general it seems to me that the part which can be played by parents should not be underestimated: even if they do not themselves embark on a full training programme they can spend time – perhaps 10 to 20 minutes each evening – 'going over' material which has been supplied by the specialist teacher.

(2) In many cases it may be helpful if the child receives 20-25 minutes' tuition per day four or five times a week.

In practice, because of difficulties over travelling, this is not always possible. As an absolute minimum one must insist on lessons once a week, and if they are as infrequent as this it is very desirable that some member of the child's family, or perhaps a trainee teacher, should provide 'revision' periods between lessons. Also there may be unavoidable breaks – because of half-term, illness, and so on – and if the weekly session itself becomes eroded, the stage may be reached where progress becomes impossible. A teacher unfamiliar with dyslexia may sometimes fail to appreciate how easily forgetting occurs.

Teachers should also be alerted to the possibility that the child needs special help with arithmetic as well as with reading and spelling.

The actual administration of the remedial teaching requires thought. There are many advantages if it is done within the precincts of the child's school: much time is saved, and teaching aids and equipment are readily available. Even more important, in my view, is the fact that the specialist teacher and the class teacher can get to know each other and work as a team. It should also be borne in mind that the child's attitude may well be affected by the way in which the situation is presented. Thus if he assumes – and no one corrects him – that he is being 'kept in' to do extra spelling (in much the same way as anyone at school who fails at a subject is 'kept in' until he achieves the required standard), or, worse still, if he regards the special lessons as in some way a punishment for failure, he may well be reluctant to co-operate. If, on the other hand, he recognises that he is being offered help so that he can overcome a handicap which everyone knows is not his fault, the situation is entirely different. Wherever the venue of the lessons, therefore, whether at school, at home, or at a special centre or clinic, it is important that this message should be brought home to him. There is no doubt at all, in my opinion, that most children are helped if one 'makes a thing' of their dyslexia rather than plays it down.

Here is a brief sketch of a boy who came to see me at

age 8 and whose dyslexia went unrecognised by the person mainly responsible for teaching him.

Case 10: Terence

I first met Terence when he was just over eight. A test carried out shortly before I saw him showed him to have a W.I.S.C. full-scale I.Q. of 124. Yet his 'reading age' (Schonell R1) was only 7.4 and his 'spelling age' (Schonell S1) 7.4 also. In addition he showed special difficulty over left and right, over saying digits in reverse order, over subtraction (where he reported that he used his toes!) and over saying the months of the year ('December, November – I'm going backwards, aren't I?' – *pause*: 'November, December, November, December, August, March, July, April – I forget') while he 'lost his place' in reciting the 4-times table.

Terence had three sisters two of whom were also found to be dyslexic. Among samples of his written work I found the following:

My Thee Wises

(1) I wisce that I gode haF a stamp awden to geeq (changed to 'keeq') my stamps in.

(2) I wisce That I gode hepe The reF you jes to Find homes For Them.

(3) I wisce That I was a powem riter and bese OF all I that I could read'.)

'My Three Wishes

(I wish that I could have a stamp album to keep my stamps in. I wish that I could help the refugees to find homes for them. I wish that I was a poem writer and best of all I wish that I could read'.)

Some time afterwards Terence's mother showed me a letter written by the senior remedial teacher for her area. It was addressed to Terence, though I suspect that it must have been intended at least in part for her own benefit.

The following are some extracts (edited so as to preserve anonymity):

'You have fallen behind (sic) in your reading and spelling. Let us be quite clear about this, Terence: there is no reason at all (underlined) why you should not catch up if you make the effort ... You should learn five words each day and you should make special note of those words which you find difficult ... '

To say that Terence had 'fallen behind' and that there was 'no reason at all' why he should not catch up shows a complete failure to appreciate what his difficulties were. I have heard of many occasions when dyslexic children were cruelly handled, and have met several who were caned for alleged laziness; but I can think of few assaults quite as cruel as the one contained in this letter.

If a teacher does not appreciate that many dyslexic children are trying desperately hard to compensate for a constitutionally-caused handicap or limitation, that teacher is best avoided.

It is also important that the time when the remedial lessons are fixed should be convenient for both teacher and child. The amount of concentration needed is such that no teacher can possibly be expected to take more than three 55-minute sessions without a break; and from the child's point of view it is most important that the lesson should not clash with his favourite out-of-school activity – whether football, swimming, canoeing or whatever it may be. It is also most desirable that the lessons should be fixed early in the day; at four o'clock in the afternoon or later one often sees signs of weariness such as stifled yawns!

In some cases it is necessary for the teaching to be done completely outside the school. Even then, it is important, at least in the case of the under-12s, that the lessons should be held during school hours: after school the child is tired, and on a Saturday morning he may be longing to go off on a bicycle ride with his friends or join in some family activity. A successful lesson is likely to be very hard work, and the conditions need to be right if the child is to give of his best. It is also very desirable that the person doing the teaching should keep in close touch with the school.

(3) What level of attainment, then, is it realistic to aim at? Perhaps the most important thing in this connection is to emphasise that the question needs to be asked. If there is no clear objective, then there can be no check on whether this objective is being achieved and indeed no adequate concern for standards. If, on the other hand, those in charge know what can reasonably be expected, then any failure to achieve it can immediately be investigated; and as a result of the experience gained it may even be possible to avoid similar combinations of circumstances in the future. A Remedial Centre which knows that it has a sizeable failure rate and is trying to improve matters deserves more respect, in my opinion, than one in which questions about failure rate are not asked. In the case of dyslexic pupils in particular, it is crucial not to underestimate what can be achieved.

In many cases an I.Q. figure may be available. I have already expressed considerable reservation about the uncritical use of I.Q. figures (see pp. 44–5). If, however, there is positive evidence of high I.Q. then it is most important not to set targets which are too low. Experience in the Gwynedd area suggests that, if the circumstances are right (for instance, if there is home support and referral by age 8½), those with a 'verbal' I.Q. on the Wechsler scale of 110 or more can be brought up by about age 12 to a reading level which is above average for their age and a spelling age of over 10, while those within the average range on the relevant Wechsler tests can be brought up to bring him up to a 'reading age' of 13 or more and a 'spelling of not less than 8½. If a pupil is believed to have the ability to do 'O' level work, every attempt should be made to bring him up to a 'reading age' of 13 or more and 'a spelling age' of 12 or more; and there may even be a case for delaying some of his examinations until this objective (or something near it) has been achieved.

(4) Well-meaning people have sometimes supposed that it does not matter what method one uses to teach a child to read and spell provided one is kind and encouraging. This has certainly not been the experience of those of us who have worked with dyslexic pupils. If a method is unsuitable then sympathy and rapport between teacher and pupil will be hard to maintain, and if I had to make the choice I should certainly recommend a brusque person using correct methods rather than a kindly person using incorrect ones.

The basic reason, it seems to me, why special methods are needed with dyslexic pupils is that such pupils seem to have some kind of special difficulty over immediate memory. As we have seen already (p. 67), they are weak at such tasks as saying digits in reverse order and repeating organised sequences such as the months of the year. Given that dyslexia involves this limitation, methods are needed for dyslexic pupils which do not overload the memory; and the objection to some of the traditional methods, such as look-and-say in the case of reading and learning words by heart in the case of spelling, is that they do precisely this. It does not, of course, follow that such methods are useless for *non-dyslexic* pupils; but whereas a person with a normal memory span can handle material designed for a person with a limited memory span, the converse is clearly not the case. Methods which are effective with dyslexic pupils may thus be effective with non-dyslexic pupils, but not necessarily vice versa.

A list of books and teaching programmes is given in Appendix II. This list is not intended to be exhaustive, but the programmes are all ones in which I myself have confidence. Those who study them in detail may notice minor differences of emphasis, but the amount of common ground becomes plain even on a casual reading. The position, I think, is this: There is plenty of scope for individual initiative by teachers, and I am not suggesting that one single 'method' is *the* right one for all dyslexic pupils; but in any programme which is to be successful, certain basic principles need to be adhered to if there is to be any progress.

These principles can be set out as follows:

(i) The pupil needs to be shown how words are built from groups of (*a*) consonants and (*b*) vowels, and should learn what are the correspondences between sounds and letters (or groups-of-letters). The programme acquires its *structure* from the fact that the teacher progressively reveals the pattern of these correspondences in the spelling system of the English language.

(ii) The pupil needs to work *systematically* through the different stages of the programme.

In the case of vowels, for instance, he first has to learn (a) the use of a single vowel for a short sound, and (b) the use of two vowels for a long sound (as in digraphs such as 'ee' and 'oa' and in the combination of a vowel with a final 'e', as in 'a-e' and 'o-e'). *Cat, box*, etc. are examples of (a); *green, boat*, etc. are examples of (b).

In the case of consonants he should be taught consonant digraphs (e.g. 'sh' and 'ch') as if they were single letters, and should be taught consonant blends (e.g. 'bl', 'cr', etc.) as combined sounds.

(iii) The programme needs to be *cumulative*. Thus there is no point in teaching longer words until the pupil has been shown how to write the syllables of which these words are made up.

(iv) The programme needs to be *thorough*, in the sense that each stage needs to be thoroughly learned before the introduction of the next stage, which in each case depends on what went before.

In brief, the basic requirement of a language training programme for dyslexic pupils is that it should be *structured, systematic, cumulative,* and *thorough.** It is particularly important that the teacher should adhere to a total programme and not simply do 'bits and pieces' in isolation.

The following, then, are some guide lines which may help

---

* I owe this wording to Mrs M. B. Rawson, former President of the Orton Society, U.S.A.

those who are attempting to decide if provision for a particular dyslexic child is adequate.

(1) Ask if the teacher has had experience of dyslexic pupils, has been on any courses for teachers of dyslexic pupils, and is willing to try to understand the pupil's difficulties.

(2) Ask if the conditions are right (time of day, place, etc.) for appropriate teaching.

(3) Ask if anyone has given thought to the question of what is an appropriate target for this pupil as far as special lessons are concerned.

(4) Ask if the methods used meet the criteria of being structured, systematic, cumulative, and thorough.

Finally, an essential quality in a teacher of dyslexic children is humility and a willingness to learn. If a teacher says to me, 'I have never yet failed to teach a child to read,' I feel uneasy even though what is said may in fact be true. In contrast, I was very happy, not long ago, to talk with a teacher whom I knew had had wide experience with some severely dyslexic children. She made no facile boasts of her successes, which in fact were many, but said simply, 'I never like being beaten.'

1987 Edition

Chapter 7

An interesting survey of the various teaching schemes for dyslexic children has been given by Naidoo (1981). It is clear from her account that although there are minor differences on points of detail there is a large amount of agreement over basic principles.

The summary of these principles given on pp. 100-101 of the present book seems to me to reflect this consensus except in one important respect. At the time when this chapter was written I had not fully appreciated the importance of what has been called 'multisensory' teaching. The pupil needs to *look* carefully, to *listen* carefully, to pay attention to his hand movements as he *writes*, and to pay attention to his mouth movements as he *speaks*. Awareness of muscular movements is called *kinaesthesis* (defined in the Shorter Oxford Dictionary as 'the sense of muscular effort that accompanies a voluntary motion of the body'); and the essential feature of multisensory teaching is that the pupil needs to be trained to form links between the visual, auditory, and kinaesthetic senses. For example the letter 'p' is not simply its written form; this written form needs to be equated with a specific sound and with specific movements of writing and speech. In addition it is now widely agreed that to teach a child the difference between 'b' and 'd' one should encourage him to pay attention to the *written* form of these two letters and *start each in a different place* – 'b' at the top and 'd' at about 2 o'clock on the loop with movement in an anti-clockwise direction. This method of teaching the difference between 'b' and 'd' is a particularly striking example of 'multisensory teaching'.

It has been possible to test statistically whether teaching based on these principles is effective. Hornsby and Miles (1980) obtained samples of children from three different centres all of which taught in this way. 107 children were studied in all, and each child's reading gain and spelling gain in the years *before the teaching started* were compared with their reading and spelling gains *during the time of teaching*. The differences were massive. The authors also found that in 85% of the cases the child's reading age during tuition kept pace with his chronological age, and there was the same figure (85%) in the case of spelling. 67% of the children achieved a reading age of 10 years or more and 83% a reading age of 9 years 6 months; the figures for spelling were 64% and 80%. Since improvement on this scale is clearly possible if appropriate methods are used there appears to be a very strong case

indeed for providing many more teachers with approp._
training.

There is also good hope that in the next decade it will be possible to write programmes of a similar kind for computers. One of the problems in this area is that the ideal computer programme would involve a speech recogniser which would pick up the pupil's inaccuracies in spoken language, and at present the large-scale provision of such devices is not feasible on grounds of cost. In addition it is important that we should all be suitably critical of untried programmes and in particular of those which do not take the distinctive weaknesses of the dyslexic into account. If these problems can be solved, however, there seems to me every likelihood of exciting developments. (For some very helpful advice in this area the reader may like to consult Hutchins, 1986).

Mention should be made at this point of a particularly interesting series of research projects carried out at Oxford University by Professor Peter Bryant and Dr. Lynette Bradley (see especially Bryant and Bradley, 1985; Bradley and Bryant, 1983, 1985). In their 1983 study 403 children aged 4 and 5 were given groups of 3 words and asked to indicate the 'odd one out' (i) in respect of initial sound, e.g. '*hill,* pig, pin', (ii) in respect of middle sound, e.g. 'cot, pot, *hat*' and (iiii) in respect of the end sound, e.g. 'pin, win, *sit*'. Three years later 65 of the children (who were still non-readers at this time) were divided into 4 groups: Group I were trained (with the help of coloured pictures of familiar objects) in phonemic discrimination; Group II received the same training but were also taught (by means of plastic letters) the shapes and names of the letters of the alphabet; Group III were given training in categorisation (e.g. 'hen' and 'pig' could both be classified as farm animals), while Group IV continued to receive normal schooling without extra training of any kind. The three groups who received training were given 40 individual sessions over a 2-year period. At the end of this period Group I and Group II were 3 to 4 months ahead on reading and spelling as compared with Groups III and IV, with Group II slightly ahead of Group

I. There was no significant difference between the scores of those in Group III and those in Group IV.

This study provides confirmatory evidence of the value of phonic training, particularly when a multisensory element is introduced, as happened in the case of Group II. It also shows that the *kind* of training is important, since if 'taking notice' of the children had been the decisive factor there would have been a similar improvement in Group III.

The fact that such methods are likely to be effective with the children whose difficulties are described in this book does not, of course, rule out the use of other methods in the case of children whose reading difficulties are of a different kind. It is confusing, of course, if these other poor readers are also described as 'dyslexic', but linguistic habits cannot easily be regulated. The important point is that the difficulties described in this book can properly be regarded as a syndrome (see p.12) whereas it would be quite incorrect to speak of a syndrome of 'reading difficulty' (or even of 'dyslexia' if 'dyslexia' is equated with 'reading difficulty') since reading difficulties are of many different kinds.

Among possible treatments for reading difficulty may be mentioned those described by Stein and Fowler (1985). These authors suggest that some children have reading problems as a result of failure to develop a fixed reference eye (which leads to absence of vergence control in the case of small targets). If they are then given occluding spectacles, it is claimed, the reference eye will become fixed and vergence will improve. The authors make clear, however, that this form of treatment is suitable for only a limited number of poor readers; and in view of this disclaimer it seems to me important that parents and others should not have unrealistic expectations.

It has also been suggested that changes in diet constitute a possible treatment for dyslexia. There is, of course, no doubt that certain individuals have particular dietary needs; and if a child is dyslexic it could well be wise in some circumstances to obtain advice on whether any changes in diet are necessary. It does not follow, however, that changes in diet are a distinctive treatment for dyslexia as such.

Another claim is that a person's reading will improve if he wears specially chosen tinted glasses. In my view this claim is of doubtful value. I know of no adequate statistical evidence in support of it; and if, as is suggested in Chapter 10, dyslexia is at bottom a constitutionally caused weakness which shows itself when the person is presented with symbolic material, it is hard to see how treatment of this kind at the 'optical' level could produce the necessary changes. It has also been suggested that dyslexics will read better if the text is shown to them upside down. If this were true it could be because the unfamiliarity of the material forces them to go more slowly and carefully. The evidence for its success is weak, however, and my personal advice to parents and teachers is that, for the present at least, they should stay with the established methods, viz. those that involve systematic multisensory teaching of letter-sound correspondences.

8

At the Secondary Stage

FROM the age of 11 onwards one must expect to find considerable variation in the extent to which dyslexic pupils are coping with their difficulties. Those who are severely handicapped or who did not receive suitable teaching until a relatively late stage may still be having a very hard struggle; and some of them may still be in a 'special' or 'remedial' class and be doing work which intellectually is insufficiently stimulating for them. There may be others, however, who have managed in various ways to compensate for their difficulties. This group includes those who have been lucky enough to receive highly skilled tuition, those of exceptionally high intelligence (who regularly devise ways of helping *themselves*), and those whose difficulties were somewhat milder in the first place. Most of such pupils may be reading adequately, even if somewhat slowly, and their spelling, though indifferent, may not be so far out of the ordinary as to be a major source of worry. In many cases they will have devised special mnemonics for left and right, for points of the compass, etc., and may have learned to use calculators or slide rules. As a result it is not always easy for their teachers to appreciate what a struggle they have had or the extent to which they may still be 'covering up'. One dyslexic adult has told me how at school, when her turn to read aloud in class was approaching, she would display a violent fit of coughing or make an urgent request to visit the lavatory!

Some recent research in which I have been involved (Ellis & Miles 1977) suggests that actual intake of information remains slow even among those dyslexic persons who

who have learned to compensate for their other difficulties. In one experiment, for instance, dyslexic adults were found to be slower than control subjects not only in reading prose but in picking out a particular combination of letters ('tg') from among others and in correctly identifying digits which were flashed on a screen; and it is a common experience that the time needed for a dyslexic pupil to do 'prep' in the evenings or to read up a topic for an essay or an examination is disproportionately long. Even after such effort he may turn in a very uneven performance or go 'off the rails' in some way (for example, as a result of having misread the question). For this reason it is particularly important that the ordinary class teacher at the secondary stage, though he need not be a specialist in dyslexia, should be aware of the effort involved. Otherwise it is very easy to blame a dyslexic pupil for 'lack of motivation' or 'carelessness', when in fact he has tried very hard and become discouraged. Some dyslexic pupils, too, because their sense of times and dates is shaky, may give the impression of being 'disorganised'. I remember on one occasion being very irritated with a 16-year-old girl who was reported to me as being regularly late for her special lesson and since her family could not afford the fees, the teacher's 'waiting time' was being paid for out of our own sparse funds! My irritation was lessened, however, when on one occasion she suddenly appeared an hour and a half early! It suddenly dawned on me that what she needed was help in using a watch and in achieving a better sense of time.

I should like also to record a conversation which I held recently with a 16-year-old boy whose school I was visiting. His only connection with me was that he had once attended a public lecture on dyslexia which I had given. Yet it was clear that he had made a special effort to come and talk to me, and the reason, I suspect, was to express his sheer disillusionment with one of his teachers whom he felt ought to have known about his difficulties and did not. He had been asked by this teacher, so he told me, to learn two of his arithmetical tables by heart. His report of the subsequent conversation with the teacher in question was as follows:

Himself: But I *can't* learn tables in this way; I am dyslexic.

Teacher: Don't be silly. Go and learn them.

Himself: Look – I'm dyslexic. This means it is hopeless for me to attempt rote-learning of this sort.

Teacher: Stop arguing. You'll stay here until you've learned both sets of tables.

Himself: I don't mind staying here. But it is still impossible for me to learn them.

The fact that this young man could talk freely about his difficulties was perhaps an indication that he had to some extent come to terms with them. But on his view of the situation – a not unreasonable one – he had been let down by someone whom he had wanted to trust and, worse still, he had in effect been accused of 'playing up' his difficulty when in fact it was a perfectly genuine one.

Appendix II includes some 'Do's' and 'Don'ts' which may be applicable to parents and teachers in general. In this chapter I have prepared a further series of 'Do's' and 'Don'ts' which are offered as a guide to those teachers at the secondary stage who are not dyslexia specialists but who may be puzzled by the presence of one or more dyslexic pupils in their class.

1. *Do* convey to the pupil that you understand (or are willing to understand) about the struggles which he has had.

2. *Do* listen freely to him if he wishes to talk to you about these struggles, about his early discouragements, about his attempts to 'cover up', etc.

3. *Do* work out with him further ways of compensation (e.g. devices to enable him to become better organised).

4. *Do* praise success lavishly; these pupils have experienced many years of failure.

5. *Do* take seriously comments on the part of his parents; they have lived with his dyslexic difficulties for many years,

and in some cases more than one member of the family may be affected. One has to be *very* sure of one's ground before disagreeing with parents.

6. *Do* be prepared for poor presentation and apparently 'careless' mistakes in his written work.

7. *Do* adjust your standards in considering what can reasonably be expected (and, where appropriate, check that *he* considers it reasonable).

8. If you are grading written work, *do* grade on content in the first place.

9. By arrangement with the specialist dyslexia teacher *do* help in small ways with spelling. For example you might take *one* misspelled word (or *two* at most) and compare it with other words which exemplify the same principles; e.g. if he spells *chalk* 'chork', show him *chalk, talk, walk, stalk.* Similarly he may be helped if you show him that two words are from the same root, e.g. *decide, decision,* or *image, imagine.*

10. *Do* break up all material (words etc.) into small units and let him take in one unit at a time without feeling 'hustled'.

11. *Don't* cover his exercise book with red ink; this is most discouraging!

12. *Don't* rub things off the blackboard too early.

13. *Don't* expect him to master the spelling systems of languages other than English.

14. *Don't* assume that he is trying to gain unfair advantage through 'being dyslexic'. In my experience this is extremely rare.

Our education system still makes life very difficult for the dyslexic child at secondary school; and it is important that *all* teachers – not merely those who are specialists in the teaching of reading and spelling – should be aware of the extent to which they can be of help to him if they show suitable sympathy and understanding.

1987 Edition

Chapter 8

The suggestion at the bottom of p. 106, viz. that dyslexia involves some kind of limitation in the ability to process information has turned out to be a fruitful one. There is, however, an important qualification which needs to be added, viz. that this applies only in the case of *symbolic* information. When he has to deal with 'things' – or, as one might say, 'things in the real world' – the dyslexic is at least as efficient as the non-dyslexic. For a discussion of some of the evidence in this area see Chapter 10.

With hindsight I believe that more should have been said in this chapter about the training of dyslexics in essay writing. Even when their reading and spelling are adequate they may still have difficulty in getting their ideas down on paper; and over the years I have received all too many reports of people who have appeared to have good understanding in a particular subject area yet have failed to do themselves justice in examinations. Those concerned with teaching the older dyslexic may like to consult Stirling (1985).

A further interesting finding which has come to light is that if one listens carefully to the oral language of dyslexic adolescents one can sometimes find remarkable inaccuracies and inadequacies. Stirling and Miles (1985) reported some tape recordings of the oral response of dyslexics and controls when they were asked to define a number of homophones (e.g. *peer/pier, place/plaice*), homonyms (e.g. *vice, chip*), and words with only a single meaning (e.g. *crocus*). The dyslexics were no worse than the controls at finding a second meaning for the homophones and homonyms, but they produced, among others, the following oddities:

peer/pier:	(i)	'a peer in the door'
	(ii)	'a pier is what people walk along and fishing off'
place/plaice:		'can be a plaice of fish'

vice:	'a vice is something that you give' (advice?)
chip:	'a chip is – er – you can give a chip to a waiter or something like that... you give him a chip, you sort of chip' (tip?)
crocus:	'a plant, or a game' (croquet?)

Stirling and Miles (1986) have suggested possible ways of correcting these oral inadequacies, and they call attention to the crucial importance of improving the dyslexic's oral language if he is to express himself adequately in writing.

9

Into Adulthood

IN this chapter I shall give some further indications as to
what are reasonable objectives for a dyslexic child at different ages. Clearly no unqualified answers are possible, since
individuals differ in all kinds of ways, but even rough and
approximate guidelines may be better than none at all.

Our present experience suggests that, if a child of average
general ability is found to be dyslexic, special teaching in
reading and spelling should start when he is aged around
7½ years old. If he receives two (or even three) years of
such teaching there is a reasonable chance that, by the time
he reaches the secondary school stage at age 11, his reading
level will be not far short of the norm for his age. Spelling
may inevitably be somewhat behind, but with suitable teaching the gap need not be all that wide. In quite a number of
cases, his arithmetic may need special help, too. If by the
age of 9 or 10 he is brought to the stage where he can read
books for pleasure and is no longer put off by them, one
has good grounds for satisfaction.

As has been pointed out already (Chapter 2 and Chapter
7), it is perhaps wise not to attach undue weight to an I.Q.
figure. Equally, however, it would be wrong to attach no
weight to it at all. Given the educational system as it is at
present, an I.Q. figure provides some kind of indication of
whether a child is likely to succeed in academic subjects.
Even in the case of a dyslexic child the figure is still a rough
guide, despite the fact that the situation is complicated by a
larger number of unknowns. It is, I think, essential to take
into account not the 'composite' I.Q. figure but rather the
child's performance on those items which present no special

difficulty for dyslexic children, though one must also re-member that for the dyslexic child there are extra obstacles to be overcome. If the I.Q. figure is no more than average, I do not say that courses with an academic bias are impos-sible (I question the wisdom of saying that anything in the educational field is impossible until one has explored many different methods over a long period of time), but at least they are likely to be very difficult. Also the less intelligent dyslexic children will be less able to show ingenuity in com-pensating for their weaknesses. With an I.Q. figure of, say, 115 and upwards, however, there seems to me every case for giving a dyslexic child the chance to do academic courses, provided one does not press him to continue with them if they are too much of an effort and provided one does not expect too much too soon. In my experience many bright dyslexic children are glad to do academic work, and when the nature of their handicap has been explained to them many of them are perfectly willing to make the extra effort.

With older dyslexic children and dyslexic adults a test which I have found useful is the Advanced Matrices by J. C. Raven (1965). It does not call for reading, memorising or acquired knowledge. What is needed is that the person taking the test should make a series of complex deductions, on the basis of which he has to pick out the correct pattern, from a choice of eight, for completing a matrix. I have known many dyslexic adolescents and adults who have scored very highly on this test, and there seems to me a good case for encouraging those who are successful to proceed with academic-type courses.

I have met quite a number of dyslexic children who were gifted at art and a small number – not, of course, the clumsy ones – who were gifted at ballet. Some, too, have been promising musicians, though in that case they should be warned not to be too discouraged if in the early stages reading notes from a musical stave presents some difficulty. A taste of success in *any* field, whether in art, music, sport or elsewhere, is likely to give a much-needed boost to morale, and it is very desirable that a dyslexic child should be given the opportunity to embark upon these activities if he so wishes.

It is not unusual for those with dyslexia to be 'behind the clock' in passing examinations. To obtain passes at 'O' level at age 17 and above is by no means uncommon, while those who go on to 'A' level may be aged 20 or more before they are successful.

It is quite possible for a gifted dyslexic child eventually to reach university, and my experience is that those who have won through to this extent against the educational system are those of high stability and determination. The evidence suggests that such people may still be slower readers than their non-dyslexic colleagues and hence take a longer time to cover assignments, carry out a survey of relevant literature and so on. There is no doubt at all, however, that it is possible for those with dyslexia to achieve real distinction. I know of several successful doctors who have been dyslexic, of a highly successful actress, and of a university lecturer in English. There is, too, Alex's father (pp. 74-75) who is a university lecturer in physics. The people concerned were, I am sure, of very high ability, but success at this level is certainly not impossible.

The examination system is unfortunately quite a hazard. Under stress a person with dyslexia may lose some of the skills which he has acquired; he may misread a question, for instance, or go 'off the rails' in other ways, and what he finally puts down on paper may be a very inadequate reflection of what he actually knows. By now, however, most examining boards have expressed willingness to make allowance for dyslexic candidates: some permit extra time; some arrange for rereading for scripts, and at least one permits the services of an amanuensis.

More needs to be done, however, in my opinion, by way of persuading society not to impose unnecessary obstacles. For entry to training in some areas, for example, it is still customary to insist on a pass at 'O' level English; and this is something which many dyslexic children find difficult to achieve (cf. the case of Robert, p. 31 *seq.*). What is important here is that acceptance for a particular job or course of training should depend only on qualifications that are *relevant*. Clearly, for example, a certain level of proficiency in reading is necessary for a nurse, a postman, a storekeeper, etc., and it is quite reasonable to turn down any applicants, whether dyslexic or not, who fail to read at the required level. What is not reasonable is to require traditional standards of literacy without detailed consideration of the needs of a particular job; a dyslexic person who fails to reach these standards may in fact be able to do the job in question perfectly well.

There are perhaps certain occupations which are particularly unsuitable for anyone with dyslexia, or at least anyone whose dyslexia has been of an appreciable degree of severity – secretarial work, for instance, or work involving written French. In both cases the time and effort involved in consulting dictionaries, checking spellings, and so on would be very large indeed, and it would be unrealistic to expect any high degree of proficiency.

For most occupations, however, the main consideration must of course be what the person wants. The extent of the handicap will vary from one individual to another, and if someone aware of his handicap and aware of the demands of a particular job and of the training needed to qualify for that job chooses to make it his objective, then in my view it would not normally be right to try to dissuade him.

Here, to finish, are four further case studies. They are presented as an indication of the kinds of thing which can happen to a dyslexic child during adolescence and early adulthood.

Case 11: Pamela

Pamela came to me at the age of 17. Her father, a doctor, wrote to me as follows: 'We would very much appreciate [an appointment] as Pamela is much distressed at her inability to spell and the fact that she has failed English Language "O" level twice.'

When I gave her the Terman intelligence test I found that she had an I.Q. of 132, and her result included passes at the top grade of 'superior adult'. Yet her school books included some misspellings of what might seem to be easy words, such as 'surtain' for *certain,* 'fearce' for *fierce,* and 'squesed' for *squeezed.* In the Schonell test, which she did for me, her mistakes included 'finacial' for *financial,* 'pliminary' for *preliminary,* 'garentue' for *guarantee,* and 'irristable' for *irresistable.* She spoke cheerfully, though not flatteringly, of teachers who 'each try their little ways' of teaching her to spell, for example by setting her to learn ten words a day. She said, however, that her mother's phonic approach, unlike other methods, had been of help and that in addition she had evolved her own techniques: 'A piece of cake is like a pie, so it is p-i-e, and peace – quiet – is the other one.'

She reported that she sometimes made mistakes in arithmetic: 'I might see 69 and write it as 96 – I'd write it correctly and say it wrong . . . I always have to say it to check I've got it the right way round' (this is my record of what she said, but I suspect that even here she has somehow confused what she meant to say). 'At one stage I used only the words I knew how to spell, but now I think "Oh blow!" to them – they can correct the spelling themselves! . . . They say you must check it, but this is hopeless. I don't know how to spell it, so I can't.'

Her original plan had been to train as a dental technician, but when she realised that her weak spelling was not just the result of stupidity she was encouraged to take 'A' levels at a technical college. I do not know if she has been successful, but on the evidence one can clearly rate her chances highly.

Case 12: Oliver

Oliver first came to me at the age of 15½. His mother had

written to me as follows: 'Though his reading ability appears quite normal, he has always had more than the average difficulty with spelling. Though this has improved he is extremely handicapped by this problem. He has had extra help both at school and at home without much real success. Oliver is now most concerned himself and is prepared to cooperate with any advice given.'

When I gave him the Terman intelligence test I came to realize what an enormous variety of different skills are required to produce the correct answers. Some of these skills Oliver possessed; but with others there appeared to be some 'block' or 'handicap', as a result of which he had to resort to roundabout methods which sometimes enabled him to reach the right answers but which carried considerable risk of error. Even within the same test item some of the component skills presented him with no difficulty while others left him struggling. For example, there is one item in the Terman test which runs as follows: 'This time you have to bring back exactly 13 pints of water. You have a 9-pint can and a 5-pint can. Show me how you can measure out exactly 13 pints of water using nothing but these two cans and not guessing at the amount. You should begin by filling the 9-pint can first . . . ' This item is difficult for many people because it calls for the ability to appreciate certain number-relationships and to select the relevant ones. Now Oliver had the special difficulty with arithmetic described on p. 53: he just did not know at a glance – as a non-dyslexic boy of his age and ability would have known – that $9 + 4 = 13$: for him that was the most difficult part of the test! The instruction book says that the subject should not use pencil or paper, but I decided to depart from this rule. After various pencil jottings he was able to decide that $9 + 4 = 13$, and with this information available he solved the 'difficult' part of the problem instantaneously! Similarly he needed his own special diagrams to work out the answer to the question, 'Which way would you have to face so that your left hand would be towards the east?', and in the end he was successful in a wide variety of items of this kind.

In general, although I was left with the impression that in many ways he was extremely bright, I found his Terman record impossible to score, since it was a patchwork of remarkable successes (including two passes at the most difficult section of all) and surprising failures, or, more strictly, failures which would have been surprising in a non-dyslexic boy of his ability.

On the Schonell word-recognition test he correctly read 73 out of the 100 words (which gives him a 'reading age' at the 12-year level), while his 'spelling age' came out at around 10½. The following were some of the spelling mistakes which I noticed in his schoolbooks: 'mtoity' for *majority*, 'argee' for *agree*, 'Tade uinions' for *trade unions*, 'temdos' for *tremendous*, 'fariself' for *for itself*, and 'pash' (with the letter r added between the s and h) for *parish*, and 'gaintic' for *gigantic*. I noticed a comment to the effect that his spelling was 'disgraceful', and I found that during the course of writing out the word 'problems' 25 times (a technique which I do not advocate) his seventeenth attempt was 'prodlems'.

When asked to point to the left side of my body as I sat opposite him, he actually swivelled round in his seat before producing the correct answer. He failed to repeat the words 'preliminary' and 'statistic' correctly; he produced the right answers in the digits reversed test but only after long delay, during which he seemed to be mentally 'writing' the digits in forward order on the paper in front of him; and he failed in his first attempt to say the months of the year. He also had special difficulty in appreciating that two words rhyme: it seemed, for instance, as though he could tell that 'head' and 'red' rhymed only by spelling them out and noting the similarities between the last few letters. (I have met this difficulty occasionally in dyslexic children but it is too infrequent to include in a list of diagnostic signs.)

His mother explained that he wanted to be a civil engineer and asked if this was 'right out of the question'. I said that I did not know and that they would have to play the situation 'by ear'. I emphasised to both of them the remarkable skill and determination which Oliver had shown in learning to compensate for his disability and gave him every encouragement to continue with these efforts. His mother told me later that his comment after his interview was, 'At last someone understands.'

When I saw him again at the age of 17 I gave him the Advanced Matrices test (see p. 143) and his score came out at exactly the average figure given for university students.

Meanwhile he had made various attempts at 'O' levels, with passes, over two years, at chemistry, history, geography, maths, physics and biology. His grades ranged from 6 to 3. His three attempts to take 'O' level English resulted, successively, in grades 8, 9, and 7. My latest information is that he has left school and been accepted on a technical course leading to the Ordinary National Diploma, with the chance of later acceptance for the Higher National Diploma.

Life has certainly not been easy for Oliver. Indeed, one of his problems when he started his technical training was whether to explain his dyslexic difficulties to the course organiser. My personal view is that if one explains things to people they are likely to be sympathetic, but this is clearly something which Oliver must decide for himself. It is not impossible that he will make a further attempt at 'O' level English, though this will depend on his eventual objectives. Clearly his difficulties with spelling and calculation are likely to remain as handicaps, but he may well achieve a great deal in spite of them. In a recent letter to me his mother spoke of his 'determination to succeed' and ended by saying 'He has come to terms with his problems and I am delighted.'

Case 13: Andrew

Andrew was 18½ years old when he came to see me. His 'reading age' came out as 12½ and his 'spelling age' as just under 9 (the maximum possible reading and spelling age for an adult being 15). Yet on the basis of intelligence tests it was clear that this relatively poor performance was not the result of general slowness, and when I checked I found some clear dyslexic signs: he had to stand and then turn round before saying which was the left side of my body as I sat opposite him; he failed to repeat the polysyllabic words 'preliminary' and 'anemone'; he failed to repeat 'four digits reversed' correctly (a task set to 9-year-olds on the Terman test); he became confused in saying the months of the year, and said that when he counted he sometimes had to use his fingers. I saw him on 3rd August and when I asked if he knew today's date he said: 'On the news it said 3rd May . . . oh, it's August . . . It's Wednesday; at least I hope it is. No, it's Tuesday – Thursday, rather.'

Spelling mistakes included: 'dughier' for *daughter*, 'egde' for *edge*, 'xpens' for *expense*, 'siret' for *street* and 'prylmanarey' for *preliminary*. A school report said that if Andrew had more confidence his work would improve, and another report said that he 'lacks effort'. One teacher had written, 'In his last English homework he spelled "tired" wrongly in one sentence and later spelled it correctly. Points to carelessness or lack of concentration.'

Andrew's father could not work because of ill health, and his parents were of very restricted means. Owing to sympathetic help from the Department of Employment and Productivity, however, it was possible to finance some training at a special school where his dyslexia was understood. I saw some of the reports from the school, which were suitably encouraging without giving false reassurance, and every opportunity was taken to commend him for the things which he had done well. At present he is learning to be a chef, and I have every hope that he will be successful.

Case 14: Phyllis

Finally, here is an account of Phyllis, who, like many dyslexic children, had an enormous struggle in the early stages.

She first came to me at the age of 10. Her I.Q. on the Terman test came out as 131, which is in the superior range, but her 'reading age' was 9½ and her 'spelling age' around

$8\frac{1}{2}$ – far below what might be expected from a girl of that ability.

This is a sample of spelling, supplied by her mother:

'Wlter rolgh was a yound menn woust to rob sponsch treasure shreps and he was a grote fo [crossed out] fat [crossed out and t altered to v] fovout of the Quen and he bunnt the fleat of sbne in the horbor, and he co [crossed out] cone book and said he hod bur the kens of spoin bred.'

She had recently been given a 'junior intelligence test' which contained a large number of written instructions. This was, of course, quite unsuitable in her case because of the time required for actual reading; and I noticed that when the written question was 'A book in which the meanings of words are found' she had written 'Becniory', which had been marked as wrong. A school report from a few years earlier said that she often wrote numerals the wrong way round, and a later report spoke of 'extreme slowness and lack of drive'. Another report said, 'I feel Phyllis has much more ability than application . . . I am still waiting and hoping that Phyllis will really wake up.'

Her parents were very much aware of her difficulties and she received special lessons from a teacher during the next year. 'She is improving steadily,' said her mother in a letter to me eight months later, 'and is now half way through *The Borrowers* . . . Her spelling is not so bizarre and obviously shows signs of improvement; she can now spell words like "once" correctly, although "are" and "out" still give trouble.'

After a change of school at age 11, she transferred at the age of $15\frac{1}{2}$ to a grammar school, where she later prepared to take 'O' levels. When I saw her at age 16 her 'reading age' was over 12 and her 'spelling age' was about $10\frac{1}{2}$. She said that she was particularly keen to do science subjects and hoped eventually to read for a degree in medicine. Needless to say, I had no hesitation in supplying her with the appropriate certificate for presentation to her examining board.

She said that she still confused the letters a and o and

occasionally made 'silly mistakes' in maths. She had given up French because of the difficulty with the spelling. Her parents showed me a recent letter home, from which the following is extracted: ' . . . as you know I was hoving trouble with the rector and I told him that I was worde blinde ond it tuoke a longe time to make him to make him there is sush a thing I think I convinsed him he said he would stort to considr my writen work insted of spelings.'

This letter, incidentally, was very much more neatly written in the earlier stages than in the later ones.

When Phyllis came to see me at the age of eighteen I gave her the Advanced Matrices test, where her score put her in about the top 15% of the *university* population – a remarkable achievement.

Her attempts at 'O' and 'A' level were not uniformly successful. At one stage she wrote to me saying she had 'a grade 2 pass in Bylogy' (sic), but had failed in Physics and English. 'I was dissopinted with my Physics but fortuntly I hove been allowed to continue with Physics "A" leval without the "O" leval. I am also doing chemistry and Bylogy at "A" leval.'

Later she wrote:

'Der Proffessor Miles

'I am sarry I hove not writen erler but I was hoping to hove some difinet news for you about what I will be doeing in October but as things go I am still waiting to here.

'My "A" leval Results are Biology A Physis A, chemesty D. The only problem is that the univisty are all ful or over full . . . he can fill his next year course with People with good grades now but the univirsty will hove to deside an thes at the end of September.'

Finally she was offered a place at a university medical school. On a recent Christmas card she wrote: 'Medicen is great fun and not too hard. I hove managed well this tearm.'

I do not think any further comment about Phyllis is needed, except to say that even those who are quite severely handicapped, as she was, can still be successful. Suitable teaching and sympathetic encouragement are, of course, essential, and it is important that *all* those who come into contact with a dyslexic child should be aware of the curious nature of the handicap. Once it is recognised, however, I am sure there are grounds for optimism. I do not wish to minimise the difficulties which confront those with dyslexia both in childhood and later, but I hope that the brief sketches in this chapter are sufficient to show the remarkable extent to which these difficulties can be overcome.

For further advice to those planning to go to college or university, see Miles & Gilroy (1986).

10
Recent Developments *

1. Attitudes to dyslexia

There can be no doubt that in the last decade public awareness of the needs of the dyslexic child has increased considerably. An important landmark was the publication in 1978 of the Warnock Report (for details see the reference section under 'Warnock'). This report included a recommendation that the existing 'categories of handicapped pupils' ('blind', 'deaf', 'educationally sub-normal, 'maladjusted', etc.) should be abolished and that in their place should be substituted the concept of 'special educational need' (20% of schoolchildren were believed to have 'special needs' of one kind or another at some stage during their school career). This recommendation, which was embodied in the Education Act of 1981, removed the necessity for any kind of legal definition of dyslexia; instead it aimed at creating the conditions in which any child who was severely retarded at reading or spelling would receive appropriate help. It has now been acknowledged by the Department of Education and Science that among children with 'special needs' are some who have 'specific learning difficulties' – an expression which for most purposes can be regarded as equivalent to 'dyslexia'.

My general impression at the present time is that the help given to dyslexic children varies in quality from one part of the country to another. There is a particularly urgent need to train more teachers for specialist work; and it is also important that class teachers sshould have at least a working knowledge of dyslexia, both so that they can suitably collaborate with the specialist teacher and, in particular, so that they are in a position to give the dyslexic child the right kind of encouragement.*

* This chapter was written for the 1987 Edition.

* Teachers interested in obtaining specialist qualifications in the area of dyslexia should ask for details from the British Dyslexia Association, 98 London Road, Reading, Berks. RG1 5AU.

2. The prevalence of dyslexia

An attempt has recently been made to determine the prevalence of dyslexia among 10-year-olds. This was the work of the Child Health Research Unit at the University of Bristol under the directorship of Professor Neville Butler. It involved a longitudinal medical and educational study of all children born in the week April 6th-11th, 1970. Data were collected in 1970 and again in 1975 and 1980. As a result of the 1980 survey scores on a variety of educational tests became available in respect of 12,905 children. One of the findings was that among the 10% of children classified as 'seriously underachieving' at either reading or spelling not less than 2% were showing two or more 'dyslexic-type' difficulties as judged by their performance on the Recall of Digits item from the British Ability Scales (Elliott et al., 1983) and on the left-right, months forwards, and months reversed items from the Bangor Dyslexia Test. (For further details of this test see below, Additional Notes to Chapter 2). A full account of this part of the 1980 survey will be found in Miles and Haslum (1986a) and a brief summary will be found in Miles and Haslum (1986b). The authors make clear in both papers that the figure of just over 2% is a very conservative one: it does not include the non-dyslexic underachievers nor does it include possible dyslexics whose underachievement was only mild or moderate.

The arguments in Miles and Haslum (1986a) are directed in part against the sceptics who say that 'no such thing as dyslexia exists'. It is of course not in dispute that some children are retarded at reading and spelling; but the use of the word 'dyslexia' is commonly understood to imply some kind of developmental anomaly – something that cannot be explained simply in terms of the normal variation between those who are good at reading or spelling and those who are less good. Miles and Haslum considered what predictions would follow if the 'normal variation' hypothesis were correct; one such prediction, for example, would be that the boy:girl ratio would be the same among the non-dyslexic underachievers as among the dyslexic underachievers. This prediction – and several others – were not in fact satisfied. They conclude on the basis of these results that the sceptic has been presented with some awkward facts which, if he is right, must somehow be explained away.

3. The nature of the difficulties

There is now wide agreement that the basic difficulty for the dyslexic lies not in visual perception as such but in the rapid processing of symbolic material. A very thorough survey of relevant evidence was carried out by Vellutino (1979), and confirmatory evidence can be found in many places, for example Legein and Bouma (1981) and Ellis and Miles (1981). Moreover, according to Liberman (1983) 'Review after review of all available research year after year to the present time . . . have all shown that most reading disabled children have no lasting problems with visual form perception, and, even more specifically, with the recognition of letters as visual forms' (Liberman, 1983). Rather than review this evidence in any detail, therefore, I shall limit myself to discussion of a small number of research findings, some of them from my own work and that of my colleagues, which illustrate this central point.

The following claims seem to me to be established: (i) when letters or other symbols are exposed for brief moments of time, for example half a second or less, dyslexics cannot 'take in' as much information as non-dyslexics; (ii) any of us is likely to be slow if we have to read unfamiliar material but dyslexics remain slow despite hard work and regular practice; (iii) when a task does not involve symbols or language it is likely to be as easy for dyslexics as for non-dyslexics; (iv) dyslexics need extra time to find the right word even in the case of familiar words such as colour names; (v) most dyslexics have problems with arithmetic.

(i) *Intake of information*

During their early investigations of this topic Ellis and Miles (1977) reported some experiments in which students were required to read several passages of prose and were also tested so as to discover what was the minimum time each of them needed in order to identify correctly strings of 5 digits flashed on a screen. The results showed that the slower readers among the students were also slower at identifying the digits. On its own this finding is perhaps not surprising. However, when the digit-identification task was given to 4 dyslexic students and was also given to 41 dyslexic children aged 10-14 and to 41 suitably matched controls, the special difficulties not only of the dyslexic children but of the 4 dyslexic students became very apparent. The following table shows the average reading speeds, in words per minute, of the different groups of students and the times needed for identification of 5 digits in the case of all 5 groups. These times are given in milliseconds (that is, thousandths of a second).

	Average reading speed (in words per minute)	Average identification time for 5 digits (in milliseconds)
Fast readers (N = 20)	305	114
Slow readers (N = 20)	181	219
Dyslexic students (N = 4)	123	450
Dyslexic children (N = 41)	–	1331
Non-dyslexic children (N = 41)	–	289

On average, therefore, the 4 dyslexic students were appreciably slower readers than were even the slowest of the non-dyslexic students. They were considerably faster than the 41 dyslexic children in identifying the strings of 5 digits but were slower than non-dyslexic children many years younger.*

* At the time Ellis and Miles (1977) thought that dyslexics might be deficient in their 'visual code store'. There is now ample evidence, however, that they are weak not at visual tasks as such but at *naming* (see section iii below). The references to the 'visual code store' in the 1977 article should therefore be

These findings make sense of the commonly reported fact that dyslexic children take a long time to copy from the blackboard. If they are slow at 'taking in' letters and numbers and can remember only a few at a time, they will need to look up at the blackboard and down to their exercise books many times in the process of copying, and on each occasion they will have to 'find the place' afresh from what no doubt seems to them a jumbled mass. The results also suggest that a dyslexic person can increase his speed of processing over the years (since the dyslexic students were appreciably faster over the digit task than were the dyslexic children) even though he still remains relatively slow. This is a point to which I shall be returning in section (ii).

Another finding reported by Ellis and Miles (1977) was that when arrays of 5,6, and 7 digits were exposed to 15 12-year-old dyslexics and 15 8½-year-old non-dyslexics matched for spelling age the dyslexics recalled considerably fewer digits per unit time than did the non-dyslexics. This is in line with the findings of Baddeley et al. (1982) that 15 dyslexics (average age nearly 13) were slower at reading aloud a list of words than 15 non-dyslexics (average age nearly 10) matched for score on a word recognition test (2 sec. per word for the dyslexics compared with 0.94 sec. per word for the younger non-dyslexics and 0.85 per word for 15 non-dyslexics matched for chronological age). Both these findings suggest that maturational lag is on its own insufficient to account for all the difficulties experienced by dyslexics and that the situation is basically unlike that in which a child is, say, late in learning to walk but afterwards walks normally. The suggestion that there is some kind of anomaly in dyslexia is correspondingly strengthened.

These two experiments exemplify a technique of investigation which has become widely practised in recent years, viz. that of comparing dyslexics with children matched for reading or spelling age and not only with those matched for chronological age. As Bryant and Bradley (1985) have emphasised, unless this precaution is taken it is always possible to argue that any differences which are found between dyslexics and non-dyslexics are simply due to lack of reading practice. There are some respects in which dyslexic children do, indeed, perform like reading-age-matched non-dyslexics (Baddeley et al., 1982), but the conditions in which they fail to do so are of particular theoretical interest.

(ii) *Can the difficulties be overcome by practice?*

Miles (1984) reports an experiment in which 3 undergraduate students agreed to practise for 20 minutes per day for a month to find out if they could improve their 'speed of processing' when arrays of 6 digits and letters were flashed on a screen. One of the students had just started to learn Russian, and in her case Russian letters were used in addition; one of the students was dyslexic. On the first day the times needed for correct responding (in milliseconds) were:

	English letters	Numerals	Russian letters
1st student (taking Russian)	725	675	1600
2nd student	775	550	–
3rd student (dyslexic)	1500	1100	–

By the end of the month the two non-dyslexic students had reduced their time for English letters and numerals to under 100 milliseconds; the student taking Russian had reduced her time for Russian letters from 1600 milliseconds to 150 milliseconds, while the dyslexic student had reduced his time for both English letters and numerals to 525 milliseconds. In general it seems likely that most people will take longer to process unfamiliar material but that the dyslexic, though capable to a limited extent of 'speeding up', remains a 'slow processer' even after a large amount of practice. At the beginning of the month this particular dyslexic student was taking about as long with the English letters as did the non-dyslexic student with the Russian letters, but at the end of the month he was over three times as slow (525 milliseconds in comparison with 150 milliseconds).*

* I should like to repeat my gratitude to Laura Ritchie, Alison Ritchie, Rebecca Mousely, and Simon Bush for their help with this experiment and to Joyce McCullogh for her help with the experiment described in the next paragraph.

In a further experiment reported by Miles (1984) dyslexic and non-dyslexic students were presented with pairs of symbols, including b/d and */+, either one above the other or one to the right of the other. Underneath the presentation was a sentence, for instance 'the b is to the left of the d' or 'the star is above the plus', and the students had to press a key indicating 'true' or 'false'. The dyslexic students were slower than the non-dyslexics in all conditions and had particular difficulty both when b and d and when left and right were involved. There can be no doubt from these results that certain difficulties experienced by dyslexics do indeed persist into adulthood despite the many ways in which they have learned to compensate.

(iii) *Performance of dyslexics at non-symbolic tasks*

The claim that dyslexics can perform as well as controls in non-symbolic tasks is supported by a large amount of evidence. (For reviews see in particular Vellutino, 1979, and Ellis and Miles, 1981. Compare also the passage from Liberman, 1983, quoted above). To avoid an excess of detail I shall limit myself to two examples.

(a) When dyslexic children were presented with two letters, one upper case, one lower case, for example Mm, Gw, and had to make a judgment of 'same' or 'different' the dyslexic children were slower and more error-prone than age-matched non-dyslexics. When two upper case letters had to be compared, however, for example RR, CT, – a task which calls for visual matching but not necessarily naming – the dyslexics were as fast and accurate as the non-dyslexics (Ellis and Miles, 1978).   (b) In a further experiment, reported in the same paper, the authors presented their subjects with a two-dimensional 'chessboard' figure in which half the squares were filled on a random basis; after varying intervals a second such figure was presented similar in all respects except that one more or one fewer square was filled in. The task for the subjects was to say whether the two figures were 'the same' or different'. Since each was exposed for only 1 second there was insufficient time for the subjects to count the squares, and it is therefore a reasonable assumption that they were relying on the visual, not the nameable, features of the patterns presented. In these conditions the dyslexics were as fast and accurate as the controls.

An important practical consequence of these findings is that no useful purpose is likely to be served by giving dyslexic children practice at shape discrimination in the hope that this will lead to easier identification of letters and numerals: since their shape discrimination is no worse than that of non-dyslexics such practice is unnecessary and in any case takes no account of their difficulty with symbols. It is a similar mistake to suppose that practice at games such as pelmanism will 'improve the memory' and hence make reading and spelling easier; in general there is no reason to suppose that exposure to material which does not have to be named will improve performance at tasks where naming is essential.

It has also been suggested that some dyslexics are 'visual learners' and some 'auditory learners'. The evidence cited above, however, does not easily square with this claim. In particular it shows that *visual tasks as such* present no special difficulty to the dyslexic. There is also evidence that the same is true in the auditory sphere. Thus Brady et al. (1983) report an experiment in which 8-year-old good and poor readers (matched for ability on a picture vocabulary test) were presented with speech sounds and non-speech environmental sounds. When suitable background noise was introduced it was found that the poor readers were at least as efficient as the good readers at perceiving the environmental sounds but that they were less efficient at perceiving the speech sounds. After reviewing these and other studies Liberman (1983) argues that the classification into 'visual learners' and 'auditory learners' is not only unsatisfactory but may even lead to faulty teaching methods. Similar views are expresssed by Elaine Miles (1981); and both she and Liberman are able to point out that a number of tests which according to their authors' descriptions are 'visual' or 'auditory' in character in fact require memory or understanding of language rather than vision or hearing as such. I myself believe that there is no particular merit in the expressions 'visual memory' and 'auditory memory': at best they do no more than indicate how the stimulus material was presented, while at worst they imply that one can have a good 'visual memory' and a poor 'auditory memory' or vice versa. What in fact is weak in the dyslexic is the memory for symbols, and this remains true whether this material is presented visually, auditorily, or through some other sense.

(iv) *Finding the right word*

There is good evidence that dyslexics are slower than controls at word finding. This has been shown, for example, in the case of the production of colour names (Spring and Capps, 1974). In addition Done (1982) showed that dyslexics aged about 14½ took longer than non-dyslexics to find the right name when presented with pictures of familiar objects.

Done followed up this discovery by interviewing 90 children between the ages of 2 and 6 in order to determine the age at which they learned the use of particular words. He presented these children with pictures of objects, for example a bicycle, an umbrella, and a windmill, and he defined 'age of acquisition' as the lowest age at which 75% of the children gave the correct answer. Now it had already been suggested (Carroll and White, 1973) that among older individuals there was a relationship between the time taken to find the right picture name and the age at which that name was acquired. Done therefore ingeniously argued that since his 14-year old dyslexics took longer to name the pictures than did suitably matched non-dyslexics they must have been correspondingly later in age of acquisition. By means of suitable statistical techniques he calculated that on average a dyslexic is likely to be 10.8 months (i.e. nearly a year) behind a non-dyslexic in the age at which he acquires a particular word.

To be somewhat speculative for a moment, it is possible that as a result of his constitutionally caused limitation a dyslexic child requires more 'exposures' to environmental sounds before they become identified as words. Now since lateness in word acquisition is associated with relative slowness in 'finding the right word' it follows that less symbolic information per unit time can get through to the dyslexic than to the non-dyslexic. This in its turn would make sense of his difficulties with all those tasks in which more than three or four symbols have to be arranged in the correct order. Spelling is clearly one such task, but the dyslexic's poor spelling is not just an isolated phenomenon: memory for digits, whether presented auditorily or visually, is another such ordering task, as is saying the letters of the alphabet or the months of the year, while the *saying* of the parts of words in the correct order may be as difficult as *writing* them. (For evidence on these points see Miles, 1983). If he is exposed to the same 'number facts' as the non-dyslexic he is likely to have fewer such facts as his disposal (see below), and this would make sense of his difficulties with subtraction and tables. Since his comprehension is adequate, one would also expect him to be able to grasp the gist of a sentence despite serious difficulty in repeating it verbatim; and this, too, is what we find (Miles, 1983). It is possible, therefore, that the root cause of the dyslexic syndrome is a relative weakness in converting environmental stimuli into symbols.

Finally, I believe it is useful to think of language skills as a kind of pyramid in which there is a successive building up of layers.* For adequate development there has to be normal hearing and normal control of the speech muscles, and if oral speech is inadequate it is inevitable that the expression of speech sounds in written form will also be affected. Difficulties with reading and spelling are of course a significant part of the dyslexic's problem, but to emphasise them at the expense of 'language skills' in general is to over-simplify what is in fact a more complicated situation. A further important fact is that many dyslexics are reported to have received speech therapy at an earlier age; and it is significant that this can happen long before difficulties with spelling have been noticed.

---

* I am grateful to Dr. Harry Chasty, of the Dyslexia Institute, for having called my attention to this important point.

(v) *Dyslexia and arithmetic*

There can be little doubt that the difficulties experienced by dyslexic children in arithmetic are 'of a piece' with their other difficulties. In particular, calculation involves the understanding of symbols, and it is very easy for a dyslexic pupil to 'miss out' when a teacher is explaining what a particular symbol means. For example considerable repetition and explanation may be needed before he appreciates that the symbol '+' indicates the operation of adding, and, similarly, if he is confronted by a combination of symbols such as ⅜ he may not appreciate that the line between the two figures indicates 'divide' or 'share'. My wife and I have met many intelligent dyslexics who even in their teens have difficulty with fractions. Relying on memory they may carry out a routine which in fact would be appropriate in quite a different context. For example, during a tour of New Zealand my wife came on the following:

$$\frac{5}{6} - \frac{1}{3} = \frac{2}{12} - \frac{5}{12} = \frac{3}{12}$$

$$\frac{7}{8} - \frac{3}{4} = \frac{3}{16} - \frac{5}{16} = \frac{2}{16}$$

$$\frac{8}{9} - \frac{1}{2} = \frac{6}{18} - \frac{8}{18} = \frac{2}{18}$$

Examination shows that this pupil was consistent in her methods in all three sums. She found a correct 'common multiple' (though not always the lowest), but she then followed a routine of cross-multiplying which would have been correct in an algebraic equation! Thus, in the first example $5 - 3 = 2$ *and* $1 - 6 = 5$ while in the second $7 - 4 = 3$ and $3 - 8 = 5$, and in the third $8 - 2 = 6$ and $1 - 9 = 8$. She also assumes that the lower number, whether it comes first or second, has to be subtracted from the higher. This was a highly intelligent piece of work, but it illustrates the danger of encouraging dyslexic children to follow a routine without understanding what they are doing.

This danger is exactly parallel to that of encouraging them to memorise spellings without giving them an understanding of the ways in which speech sounds are represented by letters.

Similarly, just as dyslexics have fewer words at their disposal which they can read at sight, so also they possess fewer 'number facts'.* This was brought home to me recently during the course of a conversation with a dyslexic undergraduate, who told me that she did not know 'immediately' that 6 added to 7 was 13 but had a strategy for working it out.

Here is no place to discuss teaching techniques. I am in little doubt, however, that the same principles that have been found to be effective in the teaching of reading and spelling will also need to be followed in the teaching of arithmetic. Just as one can show a dyslexic pupil how the English writing system works, for example, by indicating what job is done by consonants, vowels, suffixes such as '-ing' and 'ed', punctuation marks, etc., similarly one can show what job is done by symbols such as '$\div$', '$-$', and the like by confronting him with real-life situations which involve sharing, taking away, etc. Basically one needs to develop conceptual understanding – an area where he is likely to be strong – and reduce to a minimum the amount of rote learning of symbolic material. It also needs to be made clear to the dyslexic who claims to be 'no good at maths' that there is an important difference between calculation on the one hand, which is something which he will find difficult but which will assume less importance as he grows older, and grasp of mathematical principles, which is something at which he may well be highly successful. (For evidence that some dyslexics can excel in mathematics see Steeves, 1983).

An exciting new development has recently been pioneered by Bath, Chinn, and Knox (1986) in which they call attention to children's contrasting styles in mathematics. Those showing the two different extremes of style are described as 'inchworms'

* Some research confirming this point has recently been carried out by my two colleagues, Rosalind Pritchard and Louise Wales. We hope to publish details at a later date.

and 'grasshoppers'. An 'inchworm' is one who proceeds step by step along a 'safe' path. For example, if the sum is $98 + 57$ he will follow standard procedure by setting out:

$$\begin{array}{r} 98 \\ \underline{57} \end{array}$$

He will then add 8 and 7, carry 1 and finally add 1, 9, and 5, to give 155 in all. In contrast the grasshopper may immediately notice that 98 is 2 off 100 and therefore conclude that the result must be 2 off 157, viz. 155. In this particular case there are perhaps advantages in being a grasshopper, but the 'intuitive leaps' which are characteristic of his style sometimes need checking by inchworm methods, particularly in contexts where errors are costly. The authors insist that the teaching of mathematics needs to be adapted to pupils' individual styles and that in many contexts the grasshopper can usefully be encouraged to do more 'inching' and the inchworm to do more grasshopping.

People sometimes ask whether there is a separate entity, dyscalculia, additional to dyslexia. If this were so one would then need to ask how many dyslexics were also dyscalculic and how frequently the one condition occurred without the other. I do not myself believe that there is a case for postulating two different 'conditions', *dyslexia* and *dyscalculia,* whether they are thought of as independent or as overlapping. Provided one is not misled it does no harm to describe a dyslexic person with appreciable calculation difficulties as 'dyscalculic' but equally I cannot see that it does any particular good. The important point is that dyslexia involves difficulty in dealing with symbols (or, strictly, with their acquisition and reproduction rather than with their understanding), and it would in fact be surprising if the symbols used in mathematics were in any way exceptional.

It is worth recording that, in a sample of 223 dyslexics Miles (1983) found that 199 (89.2%) came out as 'dyslexia positive' on the 'tables' item of the Bangor Dyslexia Test, with a further 14 (6.3%) showing some degree of difficulty. This particular weakness does not prevent a dyslexic from becoming a good mathematician, since all sorts of compensatory devices are available to him, such as finger multiplication (Miles and Miles, 1983) or the use of table squares or calculators. I would be surprised, however, if I met someone showing other dyslexic signs who nevertheless had had no difficulty at all over calculation.

References

(i) **Books and Articles**

Allan, B.V. (1978) *Logical Spelling.* Glasgow: Collins.

Baddeley, A.D., Ellis, N.C., Miles, T.R., and Lewis, V. (1982) 'Developmental and acquired dyslexia: a comparison'. *Cognition, 11,* 185-199.

Bath, J., Chinn, S.J., and Knox, D.E. (1986) *A Test of Cognitive Style in Mathematics.* New York: Slosson Inc.

Bradley, L., and Bryant, P.E. (1983) 'Categorising sounds and learning to read: a causal connection'. *Nature, 301,* 419-421.

Bradley, L., and Bryant, P.E. (1985) *Rhyme and Reason in Reading and Spelling.* Ann Arbor: University of Michigan Press.

Brady S., Shankweiler D., and Mann V. (1983) 'Speech perception and memory coding in relation to reading ability'. *J. Exp. Child Psychol.* 35, 345-367.

Brand, V. (1984) *Spelling Made Easy.* Baldock: Egon Publications.

Bryant, P.E., and Bradley, L. (1985) *Children's Reading Problems.* Oxford: Blackwell.

Carroll, J.B., and White, M.N. (1973) 'Word frequency and age-of-acquisition as determinants of picture-naming latency.' *Quart. J. Exp. Psychol.,* 25, 85-95.

Cotterell, G.C. (1970) *Diagnosis in the Classroom.* Reading: University of Reading Press.

Critchley, M. (1970) *The Dyslexic Child.* London: Heinemann

Critchley, M., and Critchley, E.A. (1978) *Dyslexia Defined. London: Heinemann.*

Daniels, J.C., and Diack, H. (1958) The Standard Reading Tests. London: Chatto & Windus.

Done, D.J. (1982) *A Study of Paired Associate Learning and Sequential Memory in Dyslexic and Non-Dyslexic Subjects.* Ph.D. thesis, University of Wales.

Elliott, C.D., Murray, D.J., and Pearson, L.S. (1983) *The British Ability Scales.* Windsor: NFER-Nelson.

Ellis, A.W. (1984) *Reading, Writing, and Dyslexia: a Cognitive Analysis.* London: Lawrence Erlbaum.

Ellis, N.C., and Miles, T.R. (1977) 'Dyslexia as a limitation in the ability to process information'. *Bulletin of the Orton Society, 27,* 72-81

Ellis, N.C., and Miles, T.R. (1981) 'A lexical encoding processing in dyslexic children'. In M.M. Gruneberg, P.E. Morris, and R.N. Sykes (eds.) *Practical Aspects of Memory.* London: Academic Press.

Ellis, N.C., and Miles, T.R. (1981) 'A lexical encoding deficiency I'. In G.Th. Pavlidis and T.R. Miles (eds.) *Dyslexia Research and Its Applications to Education.* Chichester: Wiley.

Galaburda, A. (1983) 'Developmental dyslexia: current anatomical research'. *Annals of Dyslexia, 33,* 41-53.

Geschwind, N. (1982) 'Why Orton was right'. *Annals of Dyslexia, 32,* 12-30.

Gillingham, A., and Stillman, B.W. (1956) *Remedial Training for Children with Specific Disability in Reading, Spelling, and Penmanship.* Cambridge, Mass.: Educators Publishing Co.

Hampshire, S. (1981) *Susan's Story.* London: Sidgwick & Jackson.

Hooton, M. (1976) *The First Reading and Writing Book.* London: Heinemann.

Hornsby, B. (1984) *Overcoming Dyslexia.* London: Martin Dunitz.

Hornsby, B., and Miles, T.R. (1980) 'The effects of a dyslexia-centred teaching programme'. *Brit. J. Educ. Psychol. 50,* 236-242.

Hornsby, B., and Shear, F. (1975) *Alpha to Omega.* London: Heinemann.

Hutchins, J. (1986) 'Using a computer with dyslexic pupils'. *Dyslexia Contact,* 5, 1, 4.

Legein, Ch.P., and Bouma, H. (1981) 'Visual recognition experiments in dyslexia'. In G.Th. Pavlidis and T.R. Miles (eds.) *Dyslexia Research and Its Applications to Education.* Chichester: Wiley.

Liberman, I.Y. (1983) 'Should so called modality preferences determine the nature of instruction for children with reading disabilities?' Paper delivered to the Second World Congress on Dyslexia, Halkidiki, Greece.

Miles, E. (1981) 'A study of dyslexic weaknesses and the conseqences for teaching'. In G.Th. Pavlidis and T.R. Miles (eds.) *Dyslexia Research and Its Applications to Education.* Chichester: Wiley.

Miles, T.R. (1982) *The Bangor Dyslexia Test.* Wisbech, Cambs.: Learning Development Aids.

Miles, T.R. (1983) *Dyslexia: The Pattern of Difficulties.* St. Albans: Granada-Collins.

Miles, T.R. (1984) 'On the persistence of dyslexic difficulties into adulthood'. In J. Bath, D.E. Knox, and S.J. Chinn (eds.) *Dyslexia: Research and Its Applications to the Adolescent.* Bath: Better Books.

Miles, T.R. (1985) 'Dyslexia: the current status of the term'. *Child Language Training and Therapy,* 1, 1, 54-64.

Miles, T.R., and Ellis, N.C. (1981) 'A lexical encoding deficiency II'. In G.Th. Pavlidis and T.R. Miles (eds.) *Dyslexia Research and Its Applications to Education.* Chichester: Wiley.

Miles, T.R., and Gilroy, D.E. (1986) *Dyslexia at College.* London: Methuen (in press).

Miles, T.R., and Haslum, M.N. (1986a) 'Dyslexia: anomaly or normal variation?' *Annals of Dyslexia* (in press).

Miles, T.R., and Haslum, M.N. (1986b) 'Evidence for dyslexia in a nationally representative sample of 10-year-olds'. *Dyslexia Contact* (in press).

Miles, T.R., and Miles, E. (1983) *Help for Dyslexic Children.* London: Methuen.

Naidoo, S. (1972) *Specific Dyslexia.* London: Pitman

Naidoo, S. (1981) 'Teaching methods and their rationale'. In G. Th. Pavlidis and T.R. Miles (eds.) *Dyslexia Research and Its Applications to Education.* Chichester: Wiley.

Neale, M.D. (1966) *The Neale Analysis of Reading Ability.* London: Macmillan.

Newton, M., and Thomson, M.E. (1975) *Dyslexia: A Guide for Teachers and Parents.* London: University of London Press. (Now Hodder and Stoughton)

Newton, M., and Thomson, M.E. (1976) *The Aston Index: A A Screening Procedure for Written Language Difficulties.* Wisbech, Cambs.: Learning Development Aids.

Pavlidis, G.Th. (1981) 'Sequencing, eye movements, and the the early objective diagnosis of dyslexia'. In G.Th. Pavlidis and T.R. Miles (eds.) *Dyslexia Research and Its Applications to Education.* Chichester: Wiley.

Pavlidis, G.Th., and Fisher, D. (eds.) (1986) *Dyslexia: Its Neuropsychology and Treatment.* Chichester: Wiley.

Pavlidis, G.Th., and Miles, T.R. (eds.) (1981) *Dyslexia Research and Its Applications to Education.* Chichester: Wiley.

Pollock, J. (1978) *Signposts to Spelling.* London: Helen Arkell Dyslexia Centre.

Raven, J.C. (1965) *Advanced Progressive Matrices.* London: H.K. Lewis.

Schonell, F.J. (1951) *Diagnostic and Attainment Testing.* Edinburgh: Oliver & Boyd.

Schonell, F.J. (1961) *The Psychology and Teaching of Reading.* Edinburgh: Oliver & Boyd.

Smelt, E.D. (1976) *Speak, Spell, and Read English.* Victoria, Australia: Longmans.

Spring, C., and Capps, C. (1974) *'Encoding speed, rehearsal, and probed recall of dyslexic boys'.* J. Educ. Psychol., 66 780-786.

Stanley, G., Smith, G.A., and Howell, E.A. (1983) 'Eye-movements and sequential tracking in dyslexic and control children'. *Brit. J. Psychol., 74,* 181-187.

Steeves, J. (1983) 'Dyslexic children with mathematical potential'. *Annals of Dyslexia, 33,* 141-152.

Stein, J., and Fowler, S. (1985) 'Effect of monocular occlusion on visuomotor perception and reading in dyslexic children'. *The Lancet,* July 13, 69-73.

Stirling, E.G. (1985) *Help for the Dyslexic Adolescent.*

Stirling, E.G., and Miles, T.R. (1985) 'Naming ability and oral fluency in dyslexic adolescents'. Paper read at Baltimore, U.S.A.

Stirling, E.G., and Miles, T.R. (1986) 'Oral language of dyslexic adolescents'. *Child Language Teaching and Therapy,* 2, 143-153

Terman, L.M., and Merrill, M.A. (1961) *The Stanford Binet Intelligence Scale.* London: Harrap.

Thomson, M.E. (1982) 'The assessment of children with specific reading difficulties (dyslexia) using the British Ability Scales'. *Brit. J. Psychol.,* *73,* 461-478. ·

Thomson, M.E. (1984) *Developmental Dyslexia: Its Nature, Assessment and Remediation.* London: Arnold.

Vellutino, F.R. (1979) *Dyslexia: Theory and Research.* Cambridge, Mass.: MIT Press.

Warnock, M. (1978) *Special Educational Needs.* (Report of the Committee of Enquiry into the Education of Children and Handicapped Young People). London: H.M.S.O.

Wechsler, D. (1976) *The Wechsler Intelligence Scale for Children.* Windsor: NFER-Nelson.

(ii) Tests

Note The tests mentioned below are those which are referred to in this book. They are in no way a comprehensive list.

A. Intelligence Tests

Wechsler, D. (1949) *The Wechsler Intelligence Scale for Children.* New York: Psychological Corporation. (A revision of this test, known as WISC-R, was published in 1976 by the National Foundation for Educational Research. Present address: Darville House, 2 Oxford Road East, Windsor, Berks. SL4 1DF.)

Terman, L.M., and Merrill, M.A. (1961) *The Stanford Binet Intelligence Scale.* London: Harrap. (The 'Terman' test is not very widely used nowadays but contains some extremely informative items, particularly at age xiv and at adult level. If these items are used separately they serve to pinpoint both the strengths and weaknesses of the older dyslexic, though it is inadvisable to 'sum' the results into an overall I.Q. figure).

Raven, J.C. (1965) *Advanced Progressive Matrices.* London: H.K. Lewis. (This test is particularly suitable for older dyslexics planning to go to college).

Elliott, C.D., Murray, D.J., and Pearson, L.S. (1983) *The British Ability Scales.* Windsor: NFER-Nelson. (This is a battery of tests which aims at determining children's abilities in a variety of areas and which also includes tests of educational attainment).

B. Reading Tests

R1 Graded Word Reading Test. (This is a test of the ability to read individual words out of context). For details see Schonell, F.J. (1961) *The Psychology and Teaching of Reading.* Edinburgh: Oliver & Boyd.

Daniels, J.C., and Diack, H. (1958) *The Standard Reading Tests*. London: Chatto & Windus. (The tests in this book are suitable for beginner readers or younger children).

Neale, M.D. (1966) *The Neale Analysis of Reading Ability*. London: Macmillan. (Separate scores can be obtained on this test for accuracy, comprehension, and rate of reading).

C. Spelling Tests

S1 Graded Word Spelling Test. (For details see Schonell, F.J. (1951) *Diagnostic and Attainment Testing*. Edinburgh: Oliver & Boyd).

The Standard Reading Tests, by Daniels and Diack, see above, also includes tests of spelling.

D. Tests for Dyslexia

Those wishing for a short screening test may like to use the *Bangor Dyslexia Test (Miles, 1982)*. This can normally be administered in under 10 minutes. A longer test, yielding somewhat different information, is the *Aston Index* (Newton and Thomson, 1976). Both these tests are available from Learning Development Aids, Duke Street, Wisbech, Cambs. PE13 2AE.

E. Test for Cognitive Style in Mathematics

Bath, J., Chinn, S.J., and Knox, D.E. (1986) *A Test of Cognitive Style in Mathematics*. New York: Slosson Inc. (This test contains a variety of items, mostly suitable for older children. Its main purpose is to distinguish those whose style is predominantly 'inchworm' from those whose style is predominantly 'grasshopper').

Recognising the Dyslexic Child

(Notes for Parents and Teachers)

A word of encouragement

Dyslexia is certainly a tiresome handicap but it need not be a major tragedy. The important thing in the first place is that the handicap should be recognised. If parents and teachers understand just what it is that a dyslexic child finds difficult they can help enormously, not only by showing sympathy and giving encouragement but in particular by arranging for suitable teaching.

Does the cap fit?

A dyslexic child differs from other children of the same age in a number of ways. These differences are not shown by all dyslexic children and they occur in a number of different combinations. The seriousness of the difficulties also varies greatly. Parents and teachers may be helped to recognise when the difficulties are due to dyslexia by asking themselves the questions which follow.

If the answer to several of the following questions is *Yes,* it is quite possible that your child is appreciably handicapped by dyslexia; and in that case the *Do's* and *Don'ts* mentioned below may be of help to you ('Several' means perhaps three or four from each section.)

---

* This Appendix has been published as a separate booklet by the Dyslexia Institute. Copies are obtainable from *The Dyslexia Institute, 133 Gresham Road, Staines, Middlesex.* I am grateful to Dr. A. White Franklin, Mr. G. W. S. Gray, and Mrs. S. Naidoo for their help with its preparation.

So ask yourself:

(If he* is aged about 8½ or under)
1. Is he still having particular difficulty with reading?
2. Is he still having particular difficulty with spelling?
3. Does this *surprise* you?
4. Do you get the impression that in matters not connected with reading and spelling he is alert and bright?
5. Does he put figures the wrong way round, e.g. 15 for 51 and ᄃ for 5?
6. Does he put other things the wrong way round, e.g. b and d?
7. In calculations does he need to use bricks or his fingers or marks on paper to help him?
8. Does he have unusual difficulty in remembering arithmetical tables?
9. Was he late in speaking?
10. Is he unusually clumsy?†

(If he is aged 8½ to 12)
11. Does he still make apparently 'careless' mistakes in reading?
12. Does he still make strange spelling mistakes?
13. Does he sometimes leave letters out of a word?
14. Does he sometimes put letters in the wrong order?
15. Is he still unsure, sometimes, of the difference between left and right?
16. Are there still occasional b-d confusions?
17. Does he still find arithmetical tables difficult?
18. Does he still need to use his fingers, his toes, or special marks on paper as an aid to calculation?
19. Is it difficult for him to remember the months of the year in correct order?
20. Give him a string of three digits, e.g. 5-2-7, spoken at one second intervals, and ask him to say them in reverse order. The right answer is 7-2-5; does he ever make a mistake, hesitate or become confused?

---

* For 'he,' read 'he or she' throughout. Dyslexia appears to be somewhat more common in boys, but it can perfectly well occur in girls too.
† Some dyslexic children show clumsiness, but by no means all of them.

(If he is aged 12 or over)

21. Are there still occasional inaccuracies in reading?
22. Is his spelling still somewhat odd looking?
23. Do instructions, telephone numbers, etc. sometimes have to be repeated?
24. Does he get 'tied up' in saying long words? (Try him with *preliminary, philosophical, statistical.*)
25. Is he sometimes confused over times and dates?
26. Is a lot of checking needed before he can copy things accurately?
27. Does he still have difficulty with the harder arithmetical tables?
28. In reciting arithmetical tables in the traditional way 'one seven is seven, two sevens are fourteen', etc.) does he 'lose his place', 'skip' some of the numbers, or forget what point he has reached?
29. Present him with digits (as in 20 above) but this time give him four digits to say in reverse order, e.g. 4-9-5-8. If he is asked to say them backwards, does he ever make a mistake?
30. Does he slip back to some of his earlier habits when he is tired?

(At all ages)

31. Is there anyone else in his family who has had similar difficulties?
32. Do you have the impression that there are anomalies and inconsistencies in his performance, that he is bright in some ways but seems to have a complete or partial 'block' in others of an apparently inexplicable sort?

If for most of these questions you feel the answer is 'not particularly' then he is probably not dyslexic. If however, you feel that some of these descriptions 'fit' him then it is quite likely that he is dyslexic.

If he is dyslexic, here are some *Do's* and *Don'ts* which may be of help:

1. *Don't* simply brand him as lazy or careless.

2. *Don't* make invidious comparisons with others in his family or with others in his class at school.
3. *Don't* put pressure on him in such a way that he becomes frightened of failing or of letting you down.
4. *Don't*, without his consent, expect him to read out loud to others.
5. *Don't* expect him to learn the spelling of a word by writing it out a few times in the hope that he will remember it; he almost certainly won't!
6. *Don't* be surprised if he tires easily or becomes discouraged.
7. *Don't* be surprised if his handwriting is untidy and irregular; writing is very hard work for him.
8. *Don't* be surprised if his performance is incongruous, that is, if he manages all right on one occasion and not on another.
9. *Don't* just tell him to 'try harder'.
10. *Do* encourage him in the things that he can do well.
11. *Do* read aloud to him.
12. *Do* express appreciation of effort (e.g. commend him for attempting to write a story and, even if he has made many spelling mistakes, remind him that he has spelled plenty of the words *right*).
13. *Do* encourage him to look at words in detail, a few letters at a time.
14. *Do* discuss frankly with him the things which he finds difficult.
15. *Do* help him to recognise that there are plenty of things which he can do well.
16. *Do* encourage him to go slowly and to take his time.
17. (Most important) *Do* arrange special teaching for him (if possible on a one-to-one basis) by someone who knows about dyslexia.

Schools
If your child is at day-school, have a word with the head-master, so that between you you can make sure that special

individual teaching is given by a suitably informed and sympathetic teacher.

If you are interested in sending your child to boarding school a list of possible schools is obtainable from the British Dyslexia Association, 98 London Road, Reading RG1 5AU. You are strongly advised, however, to check *in detail* with the headmasters concerned that the school is suitable for your particular child.

Examinations

If he is entering for an examination, make sure that a certificate saying that he is dyslexic is sent to the examining board. This is normally arranged through the school.

Suggestions for Further Reading

(i) General Background

Critchley, M. (1970) *The Dyslexic Child*. Oxford: Heinemann.

Hampshire, S. (1981) *Susan's Story*. London: Sidgwick and Jackson.

Miles, T.R. (1983) *Dyslexia: The Pattern of Difficulties*. Oxford: Marston Bk Serv.

Hornsby, B. (1984) *Overcoming Dyslexia*. Paulton: Macdonald.

Thomson, M.E. (1984) *Developmental Dyslexia*. London: Whurr.

Miles, T.R. (1985) 'Dyslexia: the current status of the term'. *Child Language Teaching and Therapy, 1*, 1, 54-64.

Miles, T.R., and Gilroy, D.E. (1986) *Dyslexia at College*. Andover: Routledge.

Valuable background material will be found in *Annals of Dyslexia* (formerly *Bulletin of the Orton Society*) obtainable from 724 York Road, Baltimore, Maryland, 21204, U.S.A. Readers may also like to consult *Dyslexia Contact*, obtainable twice yearly from the British Dyslexia Association, 98 London Road, Reading RG1 5AU. In addition many useful booklets on dyslexia are obtainable from the Helen Arkell Dyslexia Centre, Fresham, Farnham, Surrey GU10 3BW. Those interested in the needs of the dyslexic adult may like to read *People with Dyslexia* (1974); this is the report of a working party commissioned by the British Council for the

Rehabilitation of the Disabled (as it then was) under the chairmanship of Dr. John Kershaw. Copies are obtainable from the Royal Association for Disability and Rehabilitation, 25 Mortimer Street, London W1N 8AB.

(ii) Research Reports and More Technical Books

Vellutino, F.R. (1979) *Dyslexia: Theory and Research.* Cambridge, Mass.: M.I.T. Press.

Pavlidis, G.Th., and Miles, T.R. (eds.) (1981) *Dyslexia Research and Its Applications to Education.* Chichester: Wiley.

Pavlidis, G.Th., and Fisher, D. (1986) *Dyslexia: Its Neuropsychology and Treatment.* Chichester: John Wiley.

(iii) Teaching Books and Programmes

Among books published in the U.K. the following are recommended:

Hornsby, B., and Shear, F. (1977) *Alpha to Omega.* Oxford: Heinemann.

Allan, B.V. (1978) *Logical Spelling.* Glasgow and London: Collins.

Pollock, J. (1978) *Signposts to Spelling.* Oxford: Heinemann.

Miles, T.R., and Miles, E. (1983) *Help for Dyslexic Children.* Andover: Routledge.

Brand, V. (1984) *Spelling Made Easy.* Baldock: Egon Publications.

Miles, E. (1989) *The Bangor Dyslexia Teaching System.* London: Whurr.

Stirling, E.G. (1984) *Spelling Check-list: A Dictionary for Dyslexics*. Llandudno: St. David's College.

Stirling, E.G. (1985) *Help for the Dyslexic Adolescent*. Llandudno: St. David's College.

One important book by an overseas author is:

Smelt, E.D. (1976) *Speak, Spell, and Read English*. Victoria, Australia: Longmans.

Reference should also be made to the comprehensive pioneer work in this field, viz.:

Gillingham, A., and Stillman, B.W. (1956) *Remedial Training for Children with Specific Disability in Reading, Spelling, and Penmanship*. Cambridge, Mass.: Educators Publishing Co.

Among the teaching materials in common may be mentioned the *Edith Norrie Letter Case* and Kathleen Hickney's *Language Training Course for Teachers and Learners*. Both these, along with most of the books mentioned above, are obtainable from Bath Educational Publishers Ltd.

Glossary

APHASIA   A condition caused by brain injury (usually as a result of an accident or a stroke) and involving disorders of thought and speech, for example the inability to 'find' the word which one wants to say.

AUTISM   A condition in which the sufferer appears to have lost contact with reality and is absorbed in fantasy.

E.E.G. (ELECTROENCEPHALOGRAM)   A device which involves the placing of electrodes on the skull and by means of which the rhythms of the brain are recorded.

I.Q. (INTELLIGENCE QUOTIENT)   A figure based on the results of a variety of tests of reasoning, etc. A child who obtains a score that is exactly average for his age is said to have an I.Q. of 100. About 16% of children of a given age-group are expected to have an I.Q. of over 115, and about $2\frac{1}{2}$% are expected to have an I.Q. of over 130.

MONOZYGOTIC   Produced by a single zygote (a zygote being the result of the union of a sperm cell from the father and an egg cell from the mother). Monozygotic (or 'identical') twins are twins born from a single zygote; and they thus have basically the same hereditary make-up. In contrast are 'dizygotic' (or 'fraternal') twins, whose heredity is no more alike than that of ordinary brothers and sisters.

READING AGE   A figure based on the child's performance on a reading test. For example, to say that a child has a reading age of 8½ implies that his attainment at reading is at the level of the average child aged 8½.

SPELLING AGE   A similar figure can be obtained on the basis of a child's performance on a spelling test.

N.B.   It is essential to remember with dyslexic children that one must expect a somewhat *irregular* performance in tests of intelligence, reading and spelling. It is therefore more important to observe their behaviour in detail than to be over-concerned with 'scoring' it.

List of Centres

England and Wales
The British Dyslexia Association, 98 London Road, Reading, Berks. RG1 5AU.

Scotland
The Scottish Dyslexia Association, The Flat, 7 Napier Road, Edinburgh. EH10 5AZ

Northern Ireland
The Northern Ireland Dyslexia Association, 7 Mount Pleasant, Stranmillis Road, Belfast BT9 5DS.

Republic of Ireland
Dyslexia Association of Ireland, 31 Stillorgan Park, Black Rock, County Dublin.

U.S.A.
The Orton Dyslexia Society, 724 York Road, Baltimore, Maryland 21204.

Australia
SPELD, P.O. Box 94, Mosman 2088, New South Wales.

New Zealand
SPELD, P.O. Box 13391, Christchurch.

Index of Names

Arkell, H. 11, 150
Allan, B.V. 137, 151
Baddeley, A.D. 128, 137
Binet, A. 18, 46
Bouma, H.
Bradley, L. 102, 128, 137
Brain, P.E.
Brand, V. 151
Brady, 131
Bryant, P.E. 102, 128, 137
Bush, S. 129
Butler, N.R. 125
Carroll, J.B. 132
Chasty, H. 133
Cotterell, G.C. 19, 85, 150
Critchley, E.A. 83
Critchley, M. 73, 75, 76, 83, 150
Daniels, J.C. 43, 143
Diack, H. 43, 143
Done, D.J. 132
Elliott, C.D. 125, 143
Ellis, A.W. 151
Ellis, N.C. 106, 126, 127, 130, 137
Fisher, D.E. 151
Fisher, V.W. 20
Fowler, S. 103
Franklin, A.W. 145
Galaburda, A.
Geschwind, N.
Gillingham, A. 152
Gilroy, D.E. 123, 150
Gray, G.W.S. 145
Hallgren, B. 73
Hampshire, S. 150
Haslum, M.N. 125
Hermann, K.
Hickey, K. 152
Hinshelwood, J.
Hooton, M. 151

Hornsby, B. 142, 150, 151
Hutchins, J.
Kershaw, J. 150
Legein, Ch.P.
Lewis, V. 137
Liberman, I.Y. 126, 130
MacMeeken, M. 76
McCullogh, J.
Merrill, M.A. 46, 60, 117, 143
Miles, E. 131, 151
Miles, T.R. 110, 125, 130, 137, 150, 151
Mouseley, R. 129
Murray, D.J. 143
Naidoo, S. 47, 145, 151
Neale, M.D. 43, 143
Newton, M. 150
Orton, S.T. 9-10
Pavlidis, G.Th. 82, 151
Pearson, L.S. 143
Pollock, J. 90, 151
Raven, J.C. 113, 143
Rawson, M.B. 100
Ritchie, A. 129
Ritchie, L. 129
Schonell, F.J. 43, 51, 60, 61, 66, 118, 143
Shear, F. 151
Smelt, E.D. 151
Steeves, J.
Stein, J. 103
Stillman, B.W. 152
Stirling, E.G. 110, 142, 151
Terman, L.M. 46, 60, 117, 143
Thomson, M.E. 150
Vellutino, F.R. 126, 130, 151
Warnock, M. 124
Wechsler, D. 46, 62, 71
White, M.N. 132
Wittgenstein, L. 58
Zangwill, O.L. 7

Index of Subjects

Advanced Matrices Test, 113, 119, 122, 143
Aphasia, 73, 76, 153
Arithmetic, difficulty with *(see also under Tables)* 14, 30, 34, 52, 59, 66
Arkell *(see under Helen Arkell)*
Autism, 68, 69, 153

Bangor Dyslexia Test, 125, 136, 144
b-d confusion: 15, 17, 22, 26, 30, 42, 50, 53, 58, 64, 67, 118
Brain damage, 68, 69, 78, 85
British Ability Scales, 144
British Council for Rehabilitation of the Disabled, 151
British Dyslexia Association, 149

Case Histories,
  1. Henry, 14, 40, 49
  2. John, 14, 19, 27, 40, 49
  3. Laura, 14, 27, 40
  4. Robert, 14, 30, 40, 74, 115
  5. Raymond, 59
  6. Elspeth, 60
  7. James, 62, 66, 68
  8. Philip 66
  9. Michael, 88
  10. Terence, 96
  11. Pamela, 115
  12. Oliver, 116
  13. Andrew, 119
  14. Phyllis, 120

Cerebral dominance *(see also under Handedness)*, 79
Clumsiness, 53, 69
Cross-laterality, 79

Days of the week, difficulty with, 61
Deep Dyslexia, 82
Diagnosis, 13, 18, 31, 40, 59
Digits reversed, difficulty with, 16, 26, 30, 42, 52, 74
Dyscalculia, 136, 137
Dyslexia:
  in adults, 59, 77, 113
  basic features, 14
  causation, 72
  as a disease, 7, 80, 85
  'doubtful cases', 57
  and examinations, 26, 36, 42
  familial incidence, 31, 54, 74
  functions of the word, 18
  as a handicap, 14, 18, 65, 72, 77, 80, 85, 93
  incidence of, 84
  and music, 113
  and sex differences, 10, 75
Dyslexia Institute, 145, 149

Electroencephalogram 80, 153
Emotional maladjustment, 78
Expectations at different ages, 146
Eyedness, 82
Eye movements, 82

Free composition, 85
French, learning of, 21, 26, 72, 115, 122.
Grasshopper style, *(in mathematics)*, 135-6

Handedness, 9, 79
Helen Arkell Centre, 151

Inchworm style *(in mathematics)* 135-6
Inconsistencies, 17, 20, 22, 147
Intelligence, 14, 23, 29, 32, 40, 42, 43, 64, 75, 85, 112

Left-right difficulties, 14, 24, 25, 31, 50, 53, 58, 62, 120

Months of the year, difficulty with, 16, 52, 61, 77, 89, 96, 118, 120
Morale factors, 19, 21, 39, 87, 108
Multisensory teaching, 102, 105

Parents, cooperation with, 19, 88, 94
Parietal lobe lesions, 76
Polysyllabic words, 16, 31, 41, 51, 62, 118, 120
Prophylactic warning, 92

Reading age 15, 43, 88, 96, 153

Schools, and the dyslexic child, 27, 91, 101, 148
  Semantic errors, 57.

Short term memory, 14, 31, 53
Slow-learning children, 63
Spanish, learning of, 22, 25, 27, 41
Speech defects 54, 69
Spelling age 15, 43, 88, 96, 98, 154
Stanford Binet Test *(see
Terman-Merrill Test)*
Subtraction difficulty with, 14
Strephosymbolia

Tables, difficulty with, 14, 26, 30, 31,
62, 79, 89, 107

Teaching sessions, organisation of, 93
Temporal ordering, difficulty with, 14
Terman-Merrill Test, 15, 46, 48, 49,
52, 60, 61, 66, 116
Twins, 74, 153

Welsh, learning of, 72
Wechsler Intelligence Scale for
Children (W.I.S.C.), 46, 52, 62,
83, 96, 98, 143